CENTRE

Australian Geographic

First published in 2000 by
Australian Geographic Pty Ltd
PO Box 321, Terrey Hills NSW 2084, Australia
Phone: (02) 9450 2344, fax (02) 9450 2990
email: books@ausgeo.com.au
website: www.australiangeographic.com.au

Managing Director: Paul Gregory
Publisher: Howard Whelan
Production/Creative Director: Tony Gordon
Managing Editor, Books: Averil Moffat

Series Concept and Cartographic Director:
Will Pringle
Design: Mark Thacker / Big Cat Design
Editor: Amanda Burdon
Production Manager: Michelle Hessing
Staff Editors: David Scott-Macnab, Andrea Smith
Picture Research: Jenny Mills
Design Layout: Cathy Campbell
Copy Editor: Scott Forbes
Proofreading, Index: Frank Povah
Editorial Assistants: Sandy Richardson, Roberta Conroy, Gillian Manning
Cartography: Laurie Whiddon, Map Illustrations, Cammeray, NSW 2062
Additional Cartography: James Austin

Copyright © Australian Geographic. All rights reserved. No part of this publication may be reproduced, stored in a retrieval system or transmitted in any form or by any means without the prior written consent of the publisher.

All photography by Barry Skipsey except pages: 31 – Australian War Memorial; 74, 79, 81, 86, 88, 123, 156, 169 – Bill Bachman; 78, 80 – Mike Gillam; 94, 122, 132 – David Hancock/ Skyscans; 59 – Rev. J. Fred Mackay; 29, 22 (S10986), 30 (JL Buckland Collection) – National Library of Australia; 68 – Olive Pink Botanic Garden; 84 – Queensland Art Gallery Collection; 133, 158 – Nick Rains; 16, 18, 113, 114, 115 bottom, 124, 159 – Dick Smith; 32, 145 – Pip Smith; 21 bottom, 89, 92, 101 bottom, 102, 120, 125, 134, 139, 165 bottom, 168 – Steve Strike/Outback Photographics; 20, 33 bottom – Richard Thwaites; 21 top – Tim Webster.

Printed in Australia by Inprint Pty Ltd.

National Library of Australia Cataloguing-in-Publication Data:

McKenzie, Kirsty.
Australian Geographic Glovebox guide: to the red centre.

Includes index.
ISBN 1 86276 046 2.

1. Australia, Central – Description and travel. 2. Australia, Central – History. 3. Australia, Central – Guidebooks. I. Skipsey, Barry. II. Brass, Ken. III. Australian Geographic Pty. Ltd. IV. Title. V. Title: Red centre. VI. Title: Glovebox guide: the red centre.

919.42

Kirsty McKenzie, Ken Brass and Australian Geographic thank the staff of the Central Australian Tourism Industry Association, particularly Diane Dancer and Nieta Milne; the staff of the Tennant Creek Regional Tourist Association, particularly Joan Small; the staff of the Parks and Wildlife Commission of the NT Geological Survey, particularly Lou Marsh, Kathy Gandolfi, Dave Fuller, Leo Abbott, Jodie Mason, Brian Prince and Ross Nowland; Jane Hodson and Tony Keys of the Central Land Council; Peter Latz; Mike Smith of the National Museum of Australia; Dennis Gee and David Young of the NT Geological Survey; Brett Galt-Smith of the Strehlow Centre; Molly Clark of Old Andado and the National Pioneer Women's Hall of Fame; Graham Short from The Gemtree; Bruce Strong from the National Trust; and Connie Spencer from Olive Pink Botanic Garden.

Cover: A majestic ghost gum stands guard at the Devils Marbles.
Page 1: The awesome domes of Kata Tjuta provide a splendid backdrop to a camel safari.
Page 2: Daytime dust storms transform the light and landscape of the Red Centre.

Ken Brass

The author of AG articles on the Tanami Desert and telecommunications in the outback, Ken Brass began his journalism career at the *Sydney Morning Herald*. He served as that newspaper's London correspondent before working for a decade on national daily newspapers in the United Kingdom. He has held writing positions on the *Australian Women's Weekly* and the *Weekend Australian* and as a freelancer now writes features and takes photographs for a number of Australian publications.

Kirsty McKenzie

Born and raised in outback Australia, Kirsty McKenzie considers herself fortunate that her writing career allows her to keep one foot in the bush. She has worked as a reporter and production editor on a number of Australian lifestyle publications and frequently works with her husband, Ken Brass. Their work has appeared in *Gourmet Traveller*, *Travel Away*, *Our House* and *R.M. Williams' Outback*. Kirsty is a regular contributor to the *Sydney Morning Herald* and has written a number of cookery and lifestyle-related books.

Barry Skipsey

It was during a working holiday in Darwin in 1977 that photographer Barry Skipsey first fell in love with the Northern Territory – a love affair that has lasted more than 20 years. From 1978 to 1980 he was the official photographer for the Territory's Chief Minister Paul Everingham, before joining the staff of the NT Tourist Commission. Barry has also worked for major metropolitan newspapers, produced the stunning images in the *Australian Geographic Book of the Red Centre* and contributes regularly to AUSTRALIAN GEOGRAPHIC, earning the coveted title of AG Photographer of the Year in 1995. When he's not roaming the Territory with his camera, Barry writes and performs bush ballads.

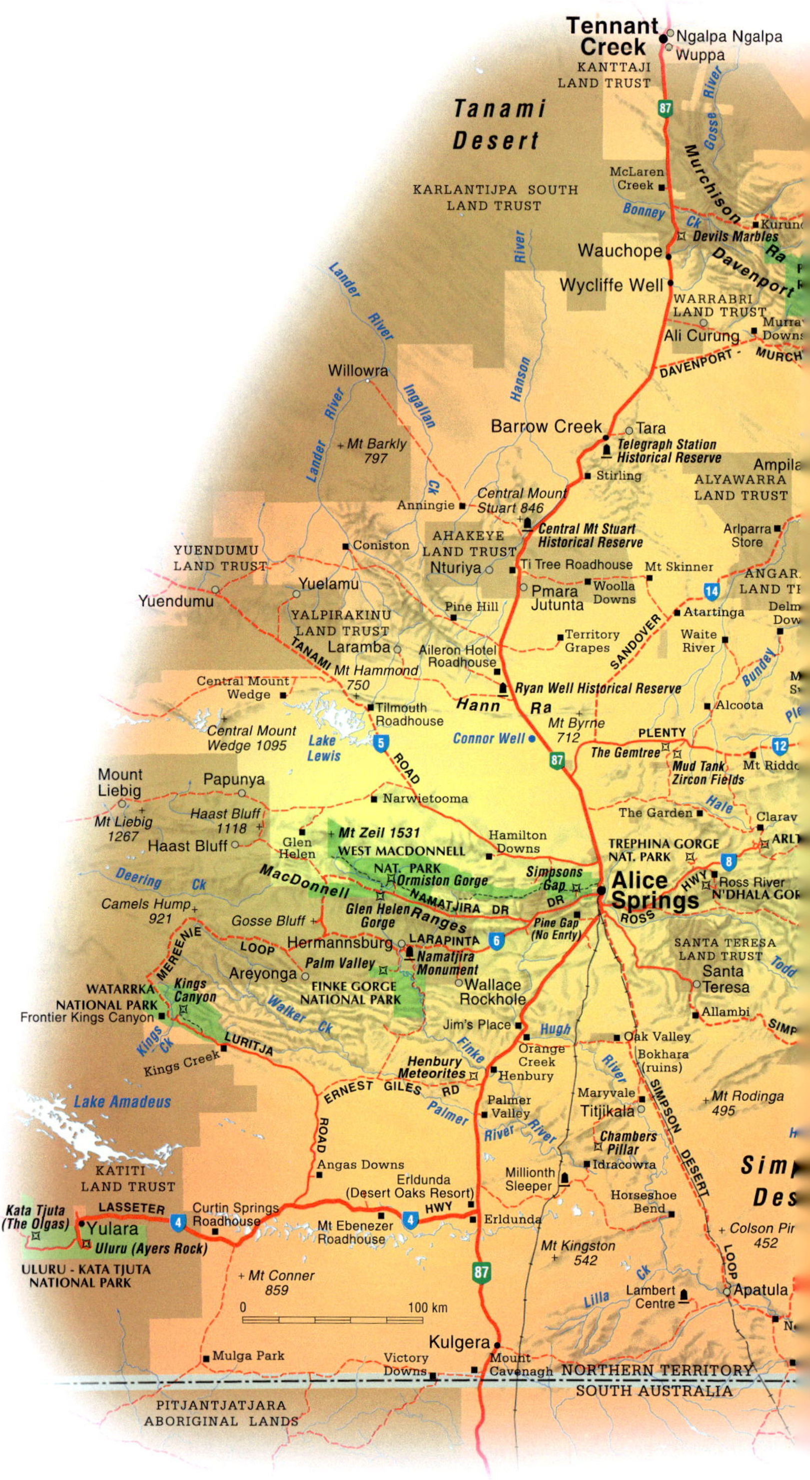

Contents

About the guide	8
INTRODUCTION	10
Overview: The Red Centre	12
Landscape and Geology	16
Aboriginal History	20
European History	26
Plants and Animals	32
Activities	38
Getting There and Getting Around	42
Essential Information	48
ALICE SPRINGS	52
WEST OF ALICE SPRINGS	74
EAST OF ALICE SPRINGS	96
SOUTH-WEST OF ALICE SPRINGS	106
SOUTH-EAST OF ALICE SPRINGS	128
NORTH OF ALICE SPRINGS	140
FURTHER AFIELD	152
SUGGESTED TOURS	160
East MacDonnell Ranges	162
West MacDonnell Ranges	164
Yulara and Kings Canyon	166
REFERENCE DIRECTORY	170
INDEX	182

About the Guide

Australian Geographic's Glovebox Guides to Australia invite you to experience this vast continent in all its wondrous detail. Compact and easy to use, they are perfect for the glovebox or daypack and a practical companion to Australian Geographic's larger travel publications.

The Glovebox Guides are divided into three sections. The first is a general overview of the area and includes information on the region's history, plants and animals, landscape and geology, activities and essential travel advice. The second section is a locality-by-locality guide to attractions and places of interest. The third – a comprehensive directory – lists all the important contacts you may need to help plan a journey or make the most of a short visit, and includes several touring suggestions.

Each section also features a series of fascinating sidebars to enhance your understanding of people, places and the landscape.

Each major locality features an overview map, and this is complemented by more detailed street and district maps introducing the sites and places of interest such as walks, lookouts, national parks and camping grounds. The places of interest described in the accompanying text are all numbered and are keyed to the relevant map.

All distances and driving times are approximate. Roads and sites are open all year round unless otherwise stated, but remember that some close on public and school holidays. For the most current information, it's best to call ahead.

Armed with this guide and an adventurous spirit, you can set off on your own journey of discovery in the Red Centre.

MAP KEY AND ABBREVIATIONS

P	Parking
✚	Hospital
🚻	Toilets
i	Information
	Caravan park
▲	Camping
	Picnic facilities
🚶	Walking track
🚴	Bicycle track
🏊	Swimming
87 4	Route numbers
✈ ✈	Airport, airstrip
▲	Historic site
¤	Point of interest
○	Aboriginal community
✳	Lookout
	Mine
▪	Homestead, Roadhouse
❸	Red numbers link map to text
⬇	Directions off map

STREET MAPS

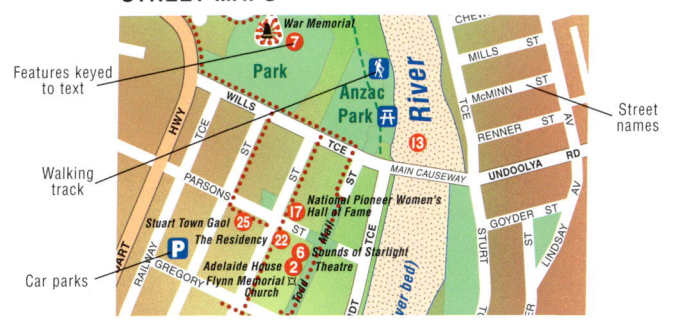

- Features keyed to text
- Street names
- Walking track
- Car parks

DISTRICT MAPS

- Physical map shows topography
- Features keyed to text

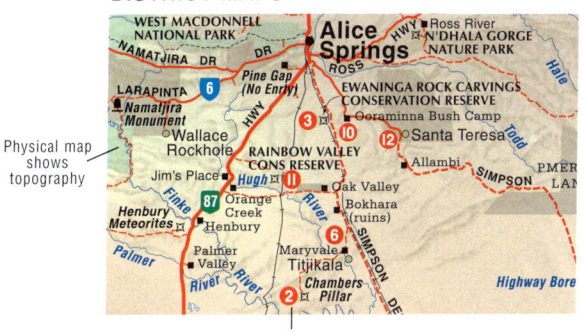

TOURING MAPS

- Suggested route
- State route number
- Points of interest
- National Park

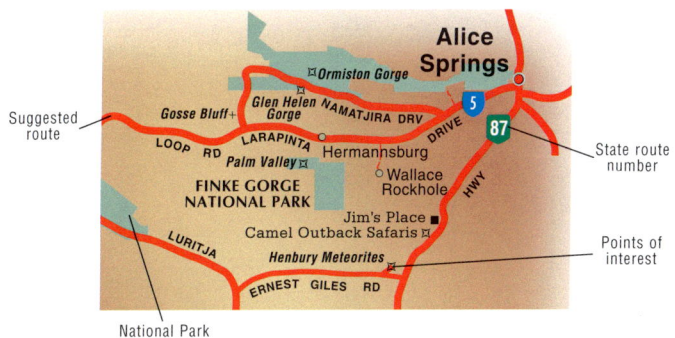

10 *The Red Centre*

INTRODUCTION

Overview: The Red Centre	**12**
Landscape and Geology	**16**
Aboriginal History	**20**
European History	**26**
Plants and Animals	**32**
Activities	**38**
Getting There and Getting Around	**42**
Essential Information	**48**

Keep an eye out for wildlife drawn to Uluru in search of water and shade.

Overview: The Red Centre

When Peter Severin and his wife Dawn took over Curtin Springs, an enormous cattle station in the south-west of the Red Centre, they received six visitors during the year 1956–57. Two were stock agents from Alice Springs, two were friends from Adelaide checking that their mates hadn't disappeared from the face of the earth and two were intrepid tourists on their way to Uluru (then known as Ayers Rock). In those days, Adelaide, 1750 km distant, was an arduous, seven-day drive away and nobody made it to Alice Springs in less than two days.

Today, Peter drives to the Alice in four hours and the road to Adelaide is a high-speed, sealed and serviced highway. In 1998, thanks to burgeoning tourism, he welcomed 300,000 people to the roadhouse and accommodation he has built near the homestead, 80 km east of Uluru. To see the nearby township of Yulara, with its permanent population of 1100 serving Uluru–Kata Tjuta National Park, it's equally hard to

Mt Conner is the least well known of the Red Centre's trio of great rocks.

Sacred site and national icon, Uluru is a place of pilgrimage for many Australians.

believe that it's just over 40 years since Jack Cotterill built his corrugated-iron "chalet" as the first accommodation (sleeping 12) there for visitors to "The Rock". Whichever way you look at it, tourism has brought massive change to Central Australia.

The 527,000 people who visited the Red Centre in 1997–98 generated $287.4 million in income and provided the greatest source of employment for the region's 36,000 residents. These tourists came to see one of the most spectacular landscapes on earth, in an area that encompasses more than 300,000 sq. km, from the Devils Marbles in the north to the South Australia border, and from Lake Amadeus in the west to Old Andado station in the east.

The Red Centre is renowned for its three great "rocks" – Uluru, rising 348 m above the surrounding plains, the less well known but equally distinctive Mt Conner, and Kata Tjuta, the highest formation at more than 600 m. Another of the area's major attractions is the mighty MacDonnell Ranges, which stretch for more than 400 km east and west of Alice Springs, rising to their highest point at 1531 m Mt Zeil. But the majesty of the Red Centre's mountains is rivalled by that of its rugged gorges and other arresting landforms including Kings Canyon in the west, the precariously balanced boulders of the Devils Marbles in the north and, in the east, the rolling sand dunes – some up to 200 km in length – of the Simpson Desert, which cover an area more than twice the size of Tasmania.

Getting out of the car invariably means getting yourself a little dusty, but the rewards can be

Guides teach spear-throwing at the Aboriginal Art and Culture Centre in Alice Springs.

immeasurable. Visitors can sample any number of splendid walks and cycling tracks, climb and swim, or hitch a ride on a camel, horse or even a Harley Davidson. This is a region that caters equally to those who choose to rough it in four-wheel-drives and swags or lounge in the lap of luxury at five-star resorts and expensive restaurants.

Ranger-guided walks and station experiences are a good way to get to know the Red Centre through the eyes of the people who live there, and a wide range of such activities is on offer. But the overwhelming majority of visitors are keen to learn about the region from its original inhabitants, the Aboriginal people. Anthropologists and archaeologists attest that Aboriginal people have lived around Uluru for at least 30,000 years. In that time, they've developed a highly complex relationship with their surroundings. They've become attuned to its climatic variations and have gained a comprehensive knowledge of its plant and animal life. In turn, the region's landscapes and wildlife have been a rich source not only of food and water but of spiritual inspiration and creation lore.

Aboriginal culture is a major drawcard for the tourism industry. The advent of self-determination and the emergence of land rights has returned ownership of almost half the Red Centre to its traditional inhabitants. Many of them now regard tourism as their children's best hope for the future.

For visitors, this means there are now numerous opportunities to develop a greater understanding of this ancient society, ranging from boomerang- and spear-throwing lessons held at Watarrka

National Park, and hunting and gathering expeditions with the Southern Arrernte at Pwerte Marnte Marnte, to discussions of bush tucker, medicine and creation stories with the Anangu, the custodians of Uluru.

The hub of tourism and other commercial activities is Alice Springs. It has grown from inauspicious beginnings as a service town for the pastoral industry to a thriving city of 27,000, with facilities ranging from a 24-hour supermarket and casino to world-class museums, galleries and nature reserves. Alice Springs Desert Park offers a fantastic overview of the amazing diversity of plants and animals that survive in this inhospitable landscape. A visit to the Royal Flying Doctor Service or School of the Air bases provides insights into the similar tenacity of remote Territorian families.

The Red Centre has a surprisingly varied climate. In summer the sun beats down fiercely and temperatures soar, often rising above 40°C. It's at this time of year when storms and rain are most common. Winters are dry but can be chilly, particularly at night.

Modern conveniences have made living with these extremes more tolerable. Electricity and refrigeration mean Peter Severin and his many visitors can wash the dust from their throats with a cold beer at the end of the day. Thanks to microwave technology, Curtin Springs even has automatic telephone services and satellite-delivered television reception. "It's hard to believe that so much has changed in one lifetime," Peter admits. "And take it from someone who lives here; most change has been for the better."

Alice Springs Desert Park provides the perfect introduction to the local environment.

Landscape and Geology

Enormous forces over millions of years have shaped the distinctive Red Centre landscape. Earth movements, vast inland seas, rivers and major climatic changes have all left their mark. Much of the terrain is ancient: granite rocks that were once part of the same mountain range as Uluru and Kata Tjuta have been dated to 1550–1150 million years ago.

Aboriginal people attribute the local landforms to giant ancestral beings of the Dreamtime, whose activities shaped the Earth's surface. Geologists offer a different interpretation. They argue that as long ago as 1900 million years, hot magma erupted from deep within the Earth, some of it filling underground chambers and some of it spilling onto the surface through

Buckling of Earth's crust created the MacDonnell Ranges about 350 million years ago.

IRON RICHES

The ruddy hue of the Red Centre's ranges can be attributed to iron oxides leached from lower layers of the original sandstones and deposited by water in the upper layers. The process can best be seen at Rainbow Valley, where the cliffs sport a reddish layer near the top, a yellow band further down, and, lower still, a white layer from which the iron has been removed.

---

volcanoes. About 30 million years later, erosion of these volcanoes deposited rocks in an adjacent sea that covered today's Tanami and Tennant Creek regions. Today, these areas are the source of the Centre's oldest dated rocks, which include the notable granite intrusion, now partly exposed, of which the Devils Marbles are a part.

For most of the period between 850 and 350 million years ago, a shallow sea covered much of the region. When it was at its deepest, probably only the area around modern-day Tennant Creek and the Davenport Range rose above the warm water. Over thousands of years, layers of sand and sediment were washed into the sea and gradually hardened to become rock. This sedimentation was interrupted by ice ages about 750 and 625 million years ago, and by two major mountain-building events approximately 550 and 350 million years ago.

The first of these periods of violent faulting and folding is known as the Petermann Orogeny. It pushed up mountains as high as the Himalaya in the southern margins of the sea, where the Petermann Ranges are today.

Prevailing winds shape the shifting sands of the Simpson Desert into parallel ridges.

The steep peaks were subsequently eroded to form coarse river gravels and sands, which in time were compressed and cemented to form the rocks of Uluru and Kata Tjuta.

The second event – the Alice Springs Orogeny – gave rise to many of the landforms that we see today. It thrust up the peaks of the MacDonnell Ranges and further raised and tilted both Uluru and Kata Tjuta. What you see now of these two landmarks are but the tips of huge deposits of sedimentary rock that may extend as far as 6 km underground.

During the more stable geological period that began around 310 million years ago, erosion and climate change assumed the major sculpting roles. Battered by wind and rain, the lofty peaks of Central Australia were gradually reduced in size, though not worn smooth – varying degrees of resistance in the underlying rocks ensured that valleys and peaks continued to form.

About 65 million years ago, Australia separated from the rest of Gondwana and began to move northward into warmer climes. As the continent drifted, the forces of nature continued to work their magic. Rounded hills were carved into ragged ranges, and rivers like the Finke and Hugh forced their way through fractures in the rocks to form caves, gaps and gorges. Eventually, the desert profile that we see today, rising from the sandplains to the summit of Mt Zeil – the highest point in Australia west of the Great Dividing Range – took shape.

Strong winds continued to gnaw at the landscape. During a dry period 18,000 years ago, which corresponded with the last ice age, these winds collected sand from the shores of shrinking lakes, scattering it downwind to form the long, parallel dunes of the Simpson Desert – the largest sand-dune desert in the world. Most of the red dunes common elsewhere in the Red Centre were also formed during this period.

EXTRATERRESTRIALS

Visitors from outer space have left their mark on the Red Centre. The rocks of Tnorala (Gosse Bluff) were not created by terrestrial pressures but thrown up by the impact of a meteorite. Central Australia's most recent extraterrestrial visitor was probably the meteor that struck the region approximately 5000 years ago, its debris forming the 12 craters at Henbury Meteorites Conservation Reserve, 130 km south-west of Alice Springs. The largest crater is 180 m wide and 15 m deep. US astronauts used these sites to simulate the surface of the Moon before the history-making landings on the real thing.

The Devils Marbles are the eroded remnants of an enormous granite intrusion.

Aboriginal History

Paintings and stencils decorate the walls of a cave in Watarrka National Park.

Aboriginal people have deep roots in Central Australia. The Anangu at Uluru say they have always been there and belong to the land through the Tjukurpa or Dreaming. Archaeological evidence goes some way to support this, showing that Aboriginal people have been in the Centre for at least 30,000 years – more than 1500 generations. During this time, Aboriginal peoples had to adapt to significant changes in climate as well as fluctuations in the availability of food and water. Although cultural links with the past were maintained, society altered considerably as time passed: populations grew, ceremonial and artistic practices became more sophisticated, and eating habits changed.

Traditional life in the bush revolved around kinship, customary law and Tjukurpa, which were interwoven with the local ecology and the environmental pulses of an arid land. During periods of rain, people would range widely across the plains collecting food and renewing their links with totemic sites. Groups would also take the opportunity to gather for ceremonies, thereby strengthening social ties. As short-lived water sources on the plains dried up, people retreated to permanent waterholes in the ranges and wells in the otherwise dry riverbeds.

Although Aboriginal peoples hunted kangaroo, emu and euro, it was small game, such as wallabies, lizards and birds, that was more common in their diet. Plant foods became increasingly important. They included tubers and yams, fruits such as bush tomato, quandong and fig, and the seeds of grasses and wattles, which were harvested and ground into flour.

Many of the rock paintings, old campsites and stone tools that visitors will come across today date back to the last few hundred years before European settlement. Rock paintings reflecting the rich oral and graphic traditions of this time can be seen at many places in the Red Centre including Uluru and Emily and Jessie gaps. Some of the designs in these works appear in the superb paintings produced by desert artists today, many of which are also reminiscent of much older rock engravings – like those at Ewaninga, and N'Dhala and Trephina gorges.

Stones like this were used to grind seeds.

There are 12 or so Aboriginal language groups in the Red Centre.

Traditional ceremonies strengthen ties between far-flung indigenous communities.

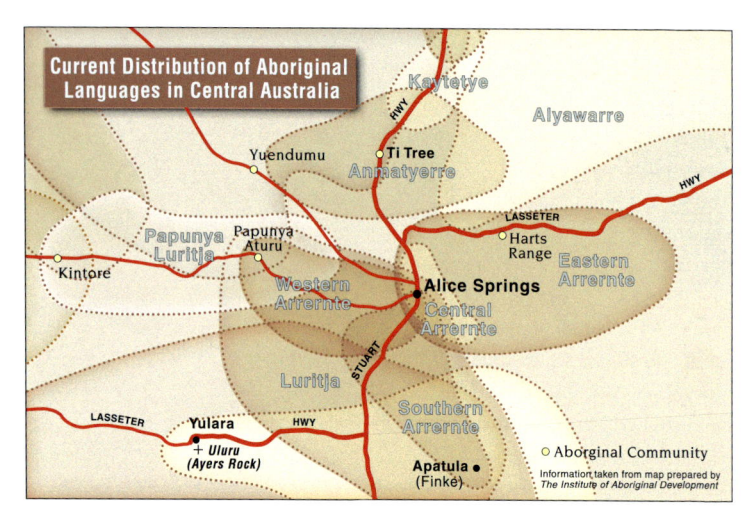

This 1870s print "The attack by the blacks upon Mr C. H. Johnstone [sic] and party at Barrow Creek, NT." by Cerberus is a graphic reminder of the early tensions.

The best known are the Arrernte, from the ranges near Alice Springs; the Warlpiri, from the north-west; and dialects of the Western Desert language – Pitjantjatjara, Yankunytjatjara, Ngaanyatjara and Pintubi–Luritja, from west and south-west of Alice Springs. The Aboriginal languages that visitors may hear in Alice Springs today – Warlpiri, Arrernte, Pintubi, Pitjantjatjara – are ancient languages as different from each other as Italian from German. But they are also living languages and developed their present form over the past 1000 years, even incorporating some

Hermannsburg's mission buildings now house a pleasant cafe and gallery.

words introduced by Europeans after John McDouall Stuart crossed the continent in 1860.

Construction of the Overland Telegraph line in 1872 cut through the heart of Arrernte territory and established a permanent European presence in the region. There were about 12,000 Aboriginal people living in the Centre at this time, but many more had already died during a smallpox epidemic that hit the region in about 1830.

Relationships with incoming pastoralists began civilly enough, but the impact of stock on the local environment was disastrous for the Aboriginal peoples' way of life, forcing them out of their traditional food-gathering areas. The severe drought of the 1890s put pressure on both indigenous peoples and settlers, and resulted in violent reprisals against Aboriginal groups for cattle-killing.

The Lutheran missionaries who founded Hermannsburg (Ntaria) in 1877 set out to create an evangelical community of self-reliant Aboriginal people in the Centre. The mission provided a safe haven during the 1880s and '90s when mounted police and punitive parties harried and murdered hundreds of Aboriginal people.

In spite of continuing tensions between Aboriginal peoples and pastoralists, a pattern of dual occupancy of the land slowly emerged. Most cattle stations relied on Aboriginal stockmen, cooks and housemaids and many of these people had traditional links to the areas where they worked. A network of government-run settlements, missions and reserves also developed across Central Australia.

In the 1950s, the Australian Government's policy of

Throughout the Centre, indigenous people now share their knowledge with tourists.

"assimilation" meant that Aboriginal people were expected to adopt a European lifestyle. Welfare agencies routinely removed children of mixed descent from their families and sent them to boarding schools or foster homes. The devastating impact of this has only recently been acknowledged, as members of the "stolen generations" have sought to re-establish contact with their families.

Aboriginal people on stations moved from rations to cash in the 1960s when they were included in industrial awards, given the right to equal wages and access to Social Security benefits. The 1960s and '70s saw other changes – most notably the lifting of restrictions on Aboriginal peoples' movements, the introduction of legal rights to property and the granting of citizenship. The land rights movement took a major step forward in 1966, when the Gurindji people withdrew their labour at Wave Hill station, in the northwest of the Northern Territory, and began a successful nine-year struggle to have their traditional ownership of the land legally acknowledged.

In 1967, a national referendum voted overwhelmingly to end constitutional discrimination against Aboriginal people. In 1975, the Tangentyere Council, an Aboriginal town-campers' association, was established to press for housing for Aboriginal people in Alice Springs, and it now plays a major role in the local construction industry. In 1976, the Federal

Government passed the *Aboriginal Land Rights Act*, which opened the way for people to reclaim traditional lands. The Central Land Council – initially a grass-roots Aboriginal organisation – was established shortly afterwards to champion Aboriginal claims to unalienated Crown Lands. The handing back of Uluru to the Anangu in 1985 represented a symbolic milestone during this period of change. Today, the Central Land Council administers an area of 775,963 sq. km. Almost half of Central Australia is under custody of Aboriginals, who make up one-third of the Red Centre's 36,000-strong population.

Since the 1940s Aboriginal people have become significant players in tourism and the arts. Aboriginal culture is a major attraction for tourists to Central Australia and opportunities to sample it generate valuable income. At Pwerte Marnte Marnte, for instance, Southern Arrernte people welcome visitors and invite them to participate in activities ranging from hunting and food-gathering to dance ceremonies.

Behind the facade of tourism, real life goes on. Aboriginal people maintain aspects of traditional life through ownership of communities and their outstations. They run cattle stations, are involved in joint ventures with mining companies, perform in rock bands, and work in the public service as well as radio and television – the Centre has its own Aboriginal broadcasting network CAAMA (Central Australian Aboriginal Media Association) and television service (Impaarja). Overall, about half the economic activity in Alice Springs in one way or another is dependent on Aboriginal people.

The popularity of Aboriginal art has increased understanding of indigenous culture.

EUROPEAN HISTORY

John McDouall Stuart had no doubt that the flag he planted in a cairn on 23 April 1860 approximately 20 km north of present-day Ti Tree marked the beginning of central Australia's history. "May it be a sign to the natives that the dawn of liberty, civilisation, and Christianity is about to break on them," he wrote portentously, adding "we can see no water".

However, Stuart's achievement, remarkable as it was, also heralded a number of endings, including the end of Aboriginal solitude and the end of the Red Centre's isolation, for his trailblazing expedition paved the way for the introduction of the Overland Telegraph Line and, subsequently, the steam train which finally puffed into the little town of Stuart, as Alice Springs was then known, in 1929.

Stuart, a lonely man with a reputation for hard drinking and a genius for exploration, made three attempts to cross the continent from south to north. He could not have foreshadowed that his final, successful crossing in 1862, when the Northern Territory was still part of New South Wales, would inspire what was to become

John McDouall Stuart's explorations paved the way for European settlement.

30,000 BP	1860	1870	1871	1872
Aboriginal occupation begins?	John McDouall Stuart arrives in the Red Centre on the first of three attempts to cross the continent from south to north	John Ross and a survey party of the Overland Telegraph Line travel through the area	An Overland Telegraph Line construction team establishes a telegraph repeater station just north of the MacDonnell Ranges at a permanent waterhole, which it names Alice Springs	The first telegraph message is transmitted from the Red Centre to Adelaide. Ernest Giles explores the Finke River and Kings Canyon; he sees Kata Tjuta, which he names Mt Olga

European History

OVERLAND TELEGRAPH LINE

Colonial Australians called it the "magic line", but there was nothing magic about the construction of the Overland Telegraph Line, which began in September 1870. The line had to cross more than 3000 km of harsh and largely unknown country, and all the equipment had to be transported overland. As well as the wire itself, this included 36,000 poles, with insulators and insulator pins, that had to be erected at 80 m intervals, and 18,000 lightning conductors. Wagons constantly hauled freight up the line and a round trip could take several months. Supplies for the 100-strong construction party included 2000 sheep, 165 horses and 210 bullocks. When the line started operating in 1872, 4000 telegrams were sent in the first year.

Australia's most ambitious engineering project – a telegraph line stretching from the populated south across the entire continent to join a submarine cable in Java that in turn connected to Europe. The following year, administration of the Northern Territory passed to South Australia and its government gave the go-ahead for the construction of the Overland Telegraph Line. Nine years later, on 22 October 1872, a message tapped out in London came down the isolated line, which largely followed Stuart's route, to Adelaide.

Land-hungry pastoralists followed the line into the Red Centre and explorers pushed further west looking for better country. Ernest Giles, during two expeditions into the region to the west of the telegraph line in 1872 and '73, put Finke Gorge (which he named the Glen of Palms), Kata Tjuta (which he named Mt Olga) and Kings Canyon on the map. Lake Amadeus and a series of smaller salt lakes prevented him from reaching Uluru, which was finally climbed and named Ayers Rock by William Gosse in 1873. Giles' companion

1873	1877	1887	1888	1926
William Gosse explores and names Ayers Rock (Uluru), and gets to Kata Tjuta before Giles can return. The first pastoralists settle in Central Australia	After a 20-month trek from Bethany, near Adelaide, German missionaries Hermann Kempe and Wilhelm Schwarz establish a Lutheran mission at Hermannsburg, 132 km south-west of Alice Springs	Gold is discovered at Arltunga in the East MacDonnells, prompting the arrival of hundreds of prospectors	The town of Stuart (later Alice Springs) is proclaimed on the Todd River, 3 km south of the Alice Springs Telegraph Station	Opening of Adelaide House, the first hospital in Central Australia. It had primitive but effective air conditioning

28 THE RED CENTRE

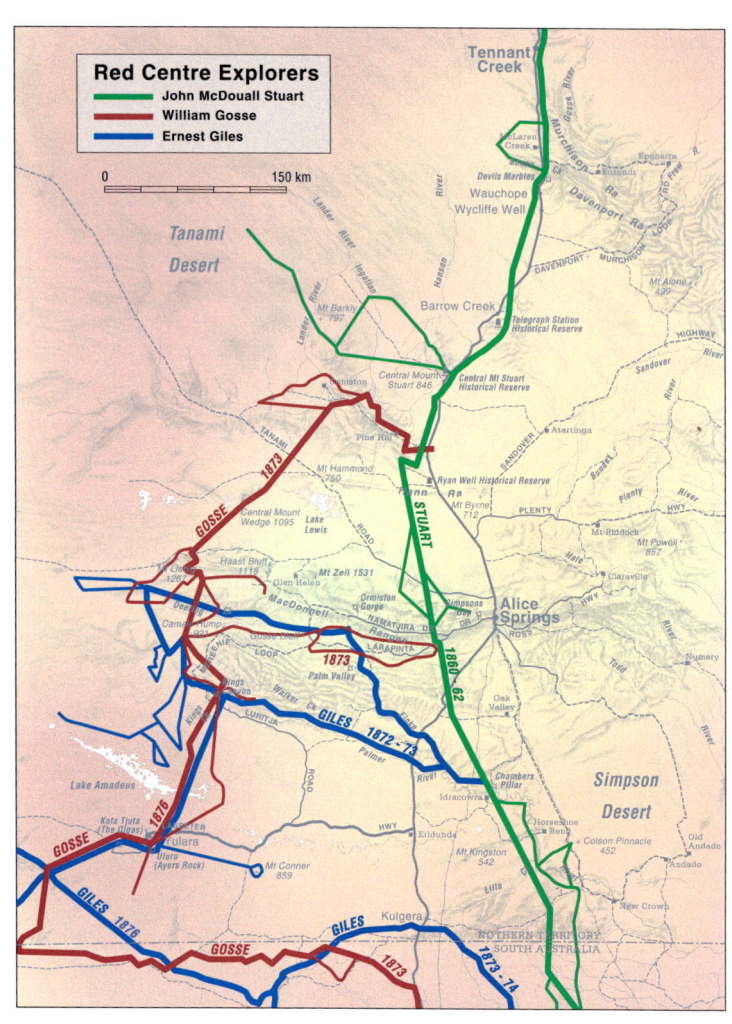

Red Centre Explorers
- John McDouall Stuart
- William Gosse
- Ernest Giles

1929	1932	1933	1935	1938
The railway from Adelaide to Stuart is completed, and a fortnightly rail service, later christened "The Ghan", begins	The Alice Springs Telegraph Station closes	The town of Stuart is renamed Alice Springs	Alice Springs becomes an overnight stop for a new two-day commercial flight from Adelaide to Darwin	Albert Namatjira has his first art exhibition and sells every painting on display

Alfred Gibson lost his life in the desert that now bears his name but Giles survived by turning back to the telegraph line. He was to reach Perth by a much more southerly route from Beltana in 1875.

The honour of being first to reach the west coast from the Red Centre went to Peter Egerton Warburton, a former officer in the Bombay Army. In one of the most hazardous journeys ever made by an Australian explorer – the team had to scoop maggots from flyblown camels to keep the beasts alive – Warburton and his son Richard, with "Afghans" and Aboriginal guides, trekked from the Centre to Port Hedland in 1873–74. In 1874, John Forrest came the other way, crossing the Gibson Desert to Oodnadatta.

As well as the telegraph line, the first settlers, stock routes, railway tracks and much of the Stuart Highway would also follow Stuart's route. Telegraph repeater stations, 11 of which boosted

> ... the horses were all floundering about in the bottomless bed of this infernal lake before we could look round. I felt sure they would be swallowed up before our eyes. We were powerless to help them for we could not get near owing to the bog, and we sank up over our knees, where the crust was broken, in hot salty mud.
> —Ernest Giles on Lake Amadeus, 1872

1939	1940–45	late 1940s	1951	1958
Australian Aerial Medical Service (later the Royal Flying Doctor Service), founded by the Reverend John Flynn, establishes a base at Alice Springs	Alice Springs becomes a major military site, especially after the Japanese begin bombing Darwin in February 1942	Len Tuit begins taking tourists to Palm Valley; within a few years his tours include Uluru	School of the Air founded at Alice Springs and starts broadcasting from the Royal Flying Doctor Service base	Jack Cotterill builds the first tourist accommodation at Uluru – a corrugated iron shed Aviator Eddie Connellan begins air services from the Alice to Uluru with his company Connellan Airways

power along the line to overcome leakage problems, became central Australia's first tiny settlements.

In the MacDonnell Ranges, survey parties found Stuart's route too rugged, so they took a different path and built a station near the river they called the Todd, after South Australia's Superintendent of Telegraphs, Charles Todd. The waterhole near the station was named for Todd's wife, Alice.

The discovery of gold at Arltunga in 1887 boosted the population of the Red Centre. The settlement called Stuart, 4 km south of the telegraph station, was surveyed the following year, but its settler population remained tiny until 5 August 1929 – the day the train came to town. The new service became known as The Ghan, after the freight-carrying "Afghan" camel trains it replaced. It spared passengers a two-week, 600 km buggy ride from Oodnadatta and brought with it modest aspirations for regional development.

Those aspirations were to be irrevocably changed by World War II. Between 1939 and 1945, The Ghan hauled 200,000 troops and 500,000 tonnes of supplies to the town, which began the war with a population of 900. Stuart had changed its name in 1933 and, as Alice Springs, became the headquarters for the Darwin Overland Maintenance Force. The population expanded further when for a time during the war the Alice replaced Darwin as administrative centre of the Northern Territory.

The soldiers left at war's end, but took with them vivid memories of the Red Centre, its raw scenery, its ancient rivers and ranges and dramatic skies, and promptly spread the word. The Chevrolet "blitz buggies" they left behind were to become rough

The arrival of the rail service in 1929 revolutionised communications.

1960	1972	1978	1980	1982
Jack Cotterill and his son Jim cut a track to Kings Canyon; the following year they begin taking tourists to the site	Noel Fullerton establishes the NT's first camel farm at Alice Springs	The NT is granted self-government	The new Ghan railway opens, with a line from Tarcoola to Alice Springs	Lutherans hand Hermannsburg mission back to the Arrernte people, traditional owners of the site

Servicemen en route to Darwin in 1944 explore the Devils Marbles.

coaches for the first wave of tourists, who thought nothing of a two-day drive from Alice Springs to camp at the base of Uluru.

By the late 1950s, so many tourists were arriving that more permanent accommodation was built at a number of destinations, although usually this was no more than a simple shed with minimal amenities. Palm Valley was the first tourist site opened to the public after World War II, and pioneer aviator Eddie Connellan commenced regular passenger services to "The Rock" from Alice Springs in 1958, less than 100 years after the first European had set foot in the Red Centre. Twenty years later, the Northern Territory became self-governing, and today the nation's rugged heart boasts an emerging tourism industry, extensive pastoralism and even a sophisticated US–Australian joint intelligence centre.

1984	1985	1992	1999	2000
The ultra-modern resort town of Yulara opens 12 km north of Uluru	Uluru–Kata Tjuta National Park handed back to the Anangu people, its traditional owners	West MacDonnell NP is gazetted when the NT government buys five cattle stations totalling 170,000 ha of land, and adds this land to the 40,000 ha of small parks in the area	The Arrernte people are granted title over most of Alice Springs. The memorial stone on John Flynn's grave is returned to the Devils Marbles and replaced by another selected by the Arrernte	The Olympic torch begins its tour of Australia at Uluru

Plants and Animals

From the air, the Red Centre can seem a parched, lifeless place. On arrival, visitors are often surprised to find a Green Centre, particularly near Alice Springs, where the adjacent MacDonnell Ranges ensure a higher and more certain rainfall than elsewhere. Although many of Central Australia's animal inhabitants are rarely seen, the calligraphy of tracks in the sand and the joyous shrieking of cockatoos at dusk are evidence that this so-called "Dead Heart" is vibrantly alive.

For most animals, survival in the Centre's three main plant communities – the desert ranges, mulga woodlands, and dunes and sandplains – is precarious. Superb adaptation is the key to success. The red kangaroo, for example, which is most common in the mulga woodlands and on the treed plains north of the Alice, reacts dramatically in times of severe drought: the male becomes sterile and the female's reproductive system shuts down. The river red gum sheds limbs to conserve water and the most common tree of the Red Centre – the mulga – channels sparse rainfall down its trunk directly to its roots.

Several species of burrowing frog avoid drought by spending

Wildflowers such as Sturt's desert pea carpet the desert with colour following rain.

BUSH TUCKER

"Great big supermarket out there", is how one Aboriginal elder described the availability of bush tucker in the Centre. For thousands of years, indigenous peoples have cooked emu, wallaby, kangaroo, goanna and other animals on hot coals, and collected edible plants, ants and witchetty grubs. They have also learned to use about 150 plant species for medicinal purposes. For example, the red sap of the bloodwood is used to disinfect wounds and native fuchsia is used to make an inhalant for treating coughs and colds. To learn more, join an Aboriginal-led bush tucker tour.

long periods underground. Having tunnelled a metre or so beneath the surface, they wrap themselves in a water-holding layer of shed skin in order to conserve moisture. There they may remain for months, even years, until heavy rain soaking into the burrow prompts them to emerge, feed and breed. As soon as the rains have passed, they again retreat to their subterranean realm.

Similarly, some plant seeds remain dormant until rain triggers germination. Then the dunes and sandplains erupt with the flowers of yellow-top daisies, papery everlastings and fluffy pussy tails. Rains also come to the rescue of the Centre's 11 species of fish, which survive in shrinking waterholes until downpours release them.

Among the best-adapted desert animals are reptiles, and hundreds of species inhabit the region. They include geckos, skinks, dragon lizards and goannas. Many have highly effective camouflage that makes them difficult to spot. Some of the adaptations are quite

Burrowing frogs conserve moisture by spending long periods underground.

WHERE TO LOOK

Life in the Red Centre can be read on the sand, with experts easily distinguishing between the tracks of a dragon and a gecko, or spotting the paired footprints of the spinifex hopping-mouse. At dawn and dusk, when most animals are feeding, crouch quietly near creeks and waterholes where you're likely to see kangaroos, wallabies and other mammals. Keep an eye out for birds and their nests – the spinifex pigeon makes a depression in the ground in the shade of a low bush or clump of grass, while the grey-crowned babbler yahoos about as it builds its dome-shaped stick nest in the fork of a tree. Walk slowly, stop frequently, sit, look and listen. Hear the "chip – chip – chip" of the white-striped mastiff bat at dusk, and use a torch to spot creatures at night.

remarkable: the thorny devil has tiny channels between its spines that direct precious moisture towards its mouth.

Bushwalkers who stray from well-worn tracks will soon become painfully aware of the Red Centre's 20 species of spiny hummock grasses – commonly known as spinifex – which dominate the desert ranges and play a vital role in plant and animal life. Ants and termites that inhabit the spinifex revitalise soil by mixing and aerating it, and by fertilising it with their excreta. In turn, these insects

Spinifex flourishes across the region.

Black-footed rock-wallabies are common in the gorges of the MacDonnell Ranges.

Plants and Animals 35

The white bark of a ghost gum stands out in sharp relief against a brilliant azure sky.

Waterholes are regularly used by wandering bird species such as the pelican.

Reptiles are abundant in the Red Centre.

become food for desert animals, including the thorny devil, which can eat 5000 ants at a sitting.

The awesome desert ranges, which lie mainly east and west of the Alice, seem so inhospitable that it's surprising to learn that they harbour the greatest diversity of plants and animals in the Red Centre. Marsupials such as the black-footed rock-wallaby are common in these areas, though declining elsewhere. Shady river red gums, coolibahs and ghost gums line the banks of the ranges' rivers. Some of the plants in the gorges and on the flanks of the hills are found nowhere else in the world. Many, including the cabbage palms of Palm Valley and the cycads of the MacDonnell Ranges and Watarrka National Park, are relicts of a bygone era when rainforests cloaked the region.

But the most abundant and obvious wildlife in the Red Centre is the birds, most often seen around permanent waterholes. Many of the 200-odd species found in the region, such as the budgerigar, pied honeyeater and crimson chat, are nomadic or migratory. At rare times when watercourses such as the Hugh, Finke, Hale or Todd rivers fill, black swans, pelicans, herons and cormorants arrive in huge numbers to feed and breed. Further afield in the woodlands, species such as the mistletoe bird, grey shrike-thrush and pied butcherbird are relatively common.

Not all the Red Centre's native animals have fared so well. Introduced species such as foxes, brumbies, rabbits and feral cats have taken a heavy toll on wildlife, particularly native mammals.

Eleven species have disappeared since European settlement in the 1870s, including the desert bandicoot and central hare-wallaby. The black-footed rock-wallaby, though often seen at Simpsons Gap, is considered vulnerable, and the bilby and mala desperately cling on in dwindling numbers. Smaller species such as the sandy inland mouse, spinifex hopping-mouse, stripe-faced dunnart and fat-tailed antechinus lead sheltered existences, either in burrows or beneath rocks and logs, emerging only at night to feed.

CAMELS

Camels – the 4WDs and road trains of their day – were brought to the Red Centre in 1871 to work on the Overland Telegraph Line. About 10,000 arrived in Australia in the 1840s, mainly from what is now Pakistan, and many more were later bred on stud farms. Superseded by motor vehicles and trains, the camels were freed, making Australia the last home of the wild dromedary. At least 70,000 now roam the Red Centre and ironically Australia exports these feral animals to countries in the Middle East.

ACTIVITIES

Central Australia's wide open spaces, its rugged, dramatic landscapes, and its dry, sunny climate make it the perfect place for outdoor pursuits of all kinds. Visitors to the Red Centre have a wide range of activities from which to choose, ranging from soft adventures for the walking-fit through to long-distance challenges for the seasoned trekker.

Hot-air ballooning: Experience the thrill of hot-air ballooning by taking a dawn flight over the region's red rockscapes. At least two companies operate out of Alice Springs. Flights usually last 30 or 60 minutes and end with a chicken-and-champagne breakfast.

Swimming is popular throughout the region, particularly during the hotter months when many Alice Springs residents eschew the town's swimming pool and head for rock pools in the gorges of the East and West MacDonnell ranges. Ellery Creek Big Hole, Ormiston Gorge, Glen Helen Gorge and Redbank Gorge are among the most popular destinations to the west of the city and Emily Gap and Trephina Gorge Nature Park are favourites to the east. At most of these sites, the water can be very cold, even in midsummer, so remember to carry a flotation device such as an innertube or air mattress.

Ellery Creek Big Hole in the MacDonnell Ranges is an ideal place to escape the heat.

Simple but satisfying, billy tea and damper is a classic bush snack.

Station stays are a good way to get to know the locals. Properties that welcome guests include Kings Creek station near Watarrka National Park, Curtin Springs near Uluru, Bond Springs, Ross River Homestead and Ooraminna Bush Camp on Deep Well station, all near Alice Springs. Along with the opportunity to sample bush hospitality and participate in station activities, many stations offer camel and horse rides. For riders preferring not to venture quite so far afield, there's a livery stable in Alice Springs.

Bushwalking: Naturally, one of the best ways to get to know the Red Centre is on foot, and bushwalkers are rewarded with many excellent tracks at Uluru–Kata Tjuta, Watarrka and (the proposed) Davenport Range national parks. For sheer variety, however, the MacDonnell Ranges are hard to beat. Walks in West MacDonnell National Park range from the short stroll along the wheelchair-accessible path to Simpsons Gap, to treks on the Larapinta Trail that could take anything from a day to a

Many outback stations offer horse rides.

Traditional outback transport carries travellers along the dry bed of the Todd River.

Gems still glitter amid the Centre's dust.

fortnight. Hikers should carry plenty of water and protect their skin with sunscreen. In the hotter months it is advisable to schedule walks for the cooler times of day. Abseiling and rockclimbing are not permitted in national parks without a permit from the NT Parks and Wildlife Commission.

Four-wheel-driving: The challenging terrain of the Red Centre provides 4WD enthusiasts with plenty of opportunities to test their skills. Among the most popular routes are the detour from the Mereenie Loop Road to Glen Helen Gorge via Tnorala (Gosse Bluff) Conservation Reserve, the Finke Gorge National Park to Watarrka track, the Simpson Desert Loop, and the track from Arltunga Historical Reserve to Ruby Gap Nature Park.

Fossicking: Rewards aplenty await diligent fossickers. In the Central Harts Range area, which encompasses the abandoned mica mines of Mount Palmer, discoveries might include garnet, tourmaline, beryl and amethyst, as well as rose, smoky, blue and clear quartz. There's still gold to be found at

Arltunga and at Warrego near Tennant Creek. Close to Alice Springs, amethyst can be found in the soil and weathered scree at the foot of the hill at Ilparpa. Permits are available from Minerals House, 58 Hartley Street, Alice Springs (☎ 08-8951 5658); or the Central Australian Tourism Industry Association office, Alice Springs (☎ 08-8952 5800); Arltunga Bush Hotel, Arltunga Tourist Drive, Arltunga (☎ 08-8956 9797); the Gemtree Caravan Park, Plenty Highway, The Gemtree (☎ 08-8956 9855) and Tennant Creek Regional Tourist Association, Battery Hill Regional Centre, Peko Road, Tennant Creek (☎ 08-8962 3388).

Cycling: The countryside lends itself to cycling and the Alice, in particular, is a good place to explore by bike. The 17 km Simpsons Gap bike path (see West of Alice Springs) is an easy day's ride. Bikes can be hired in the Alice at Centre Cycles, corner Lindsay Avenue and Undoolya Road (☎ 08-8953 2966) and Melanka Lodge, 94 Todd Street (☎ 08-8952 2233).

Camel riding: Camel rides provide an opportunity to participate in the experiences of the early settlers, many of whom relied on the "ship of the desert" for transport and freight. Lean back and lurch into the landscape at Alice Springs, Stuart's Well and Uluru. Options range from a five-minute sortie to taking a camel to breakfast, sunset, dinner … even bed, on overnight and extended treks.

Four-wheel-drive vehicles offer unlimited potential for exploration and adventure.

Getting There and Getting Around

Whichever way you travel to the Red Centre, getting there will be an adventure. It's 1490 km to Alice Springs from Darwin, 1530 km from Adelaide, 3933 km from Perth and 2958 km from Sydney. Even during a journey by air, which takes more than two hours from Sydney, there's plenty of time to contemplate the vastness of the outback. Travelling by car, particularly along one of the famous 4WD routes, you could be forgiven for thinking the journey will never end.

AIR

There are direct services daily to Alice Springs from Sydney, Perth, Adelaide, Darwin and Cairns, and daily flights (about 50 minutes) from Alice Springs to Uluru.

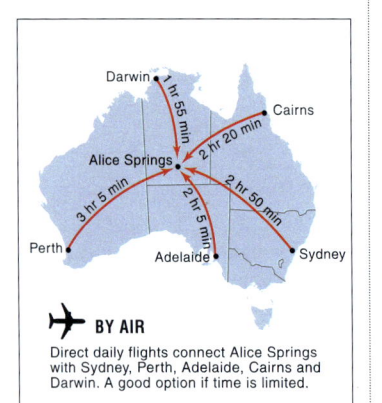

BY AIR
Direct daily flights connect Alice Springs with Sydney, Perth, Adelaide, Cairns and Darwin. A good option if time is limited.

Private coach tours are among a wide range of travel options offered locally.

A return economy airfare from Sydney to Alice Springs will cost about $1285, although discounts (sometimes more than 50 per cent) apply for advance purchase.

Alice Springs airport is 17 km from town. The Airport Shuttle Service (☎ 08-8953 0310) meets every flight and takes passengers to and from their accommodation as well as to the railway station ($9.90 single, $16.50 return). Patrons may leave their luggage at the company office, opposite the Central Australian Tourism Industry Association (CATIA) office on Gregory Terrace. Taxis and hire cars are also available at the airport.
- *Qantas bookings:* ☎ *13 13 13*
- *Ansett bookings:* ☎ *13 13 00.*

BUS

There are regular daily express services between Alice Springs and

Adelaide, Darwin and Yulara. It takes about 19 hours to travel from Adelaide to Alice Springs and about 20 hours from the Alice to Darwin. The northern service connects with the Tennant Creek to Townsville service, providing access to Queensland cities. From Adelaide, travellers can connect to Sydney and Melbourne.

A standard fare from Alice Springs to Sydney is around $200 one way or $430 return. Cheaper travel is available by purchasing passes for set kilometres, routes or number of days travel. Costs range from about $205 for a 2000 km pass to about $1660 for 20,000 km.

- *McCafferty's bookings:* ☎ *13 14 99. Terminus: Shop 3, 91 Gregory Tce, Alice Springs,* ☎ *08-8952 3952.*
- *Greyhound–Pioneer bookings:* ☎ *13 20 30. Terminus: Shop 22, Coles complex, Gregory Tce, Alice Springs,* ☎ *08-8952 7888.*

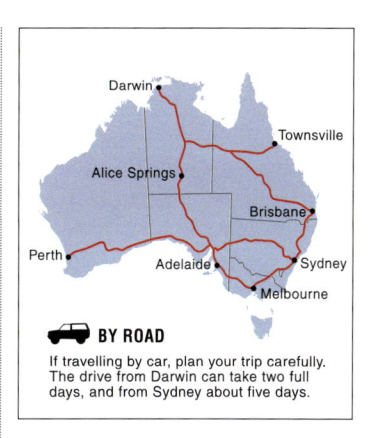

BY ROAD

If travelling by car, plan your trip carefully. The drive from Darwin can take two full days, and from Sydney about five days.

TRAIN

The Ghan operates weekly services from Sydney and Melbourne to Alice Springs and twice weekly services from Adelaide to the Alice. Billed as one of the great railway journeys of the world, the trip takes nearly two full days from Sydney. You can also put your car on the train (at a cost of $618 from Sydney to Alice

Sit back and savour the dramatic scenery – and fine cuisine – aboard The Ghan.

Springs) so that you have your own transport on arrival. One-way fares from Sydney to Alice range from $360 for a coach-class lounge chair to $890 for a first-class ensuite sleeping berth. The Alice Springs railway station is in George Crescent. Buslink (☎ 08-8952 5611) provides transfers to downtown and hotels on arrival.

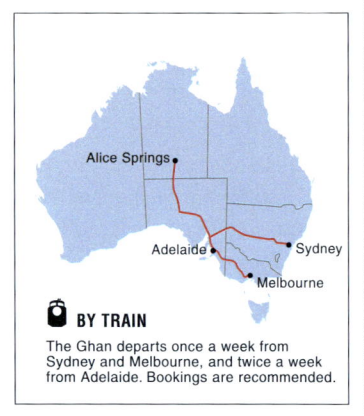

BY TRAIN
The Ghan departs once a week from Sydney and Melbourne, and twice a week from Adelaide. Bookings are recommended.

Distances between major sites are great, so allow plenty of time for your journeys.

- *Great Southern Railway (Ghan) bookings:* ☎ *13 21 47.*
- *Buslink fare: adults, $4.*

CAR
It's a long, two-day drive from Darwin to the Alice and probably the minimum time it takes to comfortably drive from Sydney to Alice, including overnight stops, is four or five days – and even that's based on an average of more than 750 km per day. For this reason, many travellers opt to take a plane, bus or train to the Red Centre and hire a car, camper or 4WD in Alice or Yulara.

Car hire companies include:
- *Hertz Northern Territory: 76 Hartley St, Alice Springs,* ☎ *08-8952 2644; Touring and Information Centre, Yulara,* ☎ *08-8956 2244.*
- *Avis: 52 Hartley St, Alice Springs,* ☎ *08-8953 5533; Connellan Airport, Uluru,* ☎ *08-8956 2266.*
- *Budget Rent A Car: 10 Gap Rd, Alice Springs,* ☎ *08-8952 8899.*

Camper and 4WD companies include:
- *Outback Auto Rental: 78 Todd St, Alice Springs,* ☎ *08-8953 5333.*
- *Britz Australia Rentals: cnr Stuart Hwy and Power St, Alice Springs,* ☎ *08-8952 8814.*
- *Apollo Motorhome Holidays: 3 Larapinta Dr, Alice Springs,* ☎ *08-8952 7255.*

ORGANISED TOURS
Packages available locally range from luxury tours including travel in air-conditioned coaches and

Air tours allow you to view and visit some of the most remote parts of the outback.

accommodation in hotels, to 4WD camping safaris, where you sleep in a tent you've pitched yourself.

Another option is to take advantage of one of the Northern Territory's air services. These include Ngurratjuta Air (☎ 08-8953 5000), which operates a postal run to remote Aboriginal communities, and Didgeri Air Art Tours (☎ 08-8948 5055), which takes travellers on tours of Aboriginal communities that produce artworks. Commercial pilot Murray Cosson (☎ 08-8952 4625) also offers a full-day air tour and "charter flights to anywhere".
● *AAT Kings Tours: 74 Todd St, Alice Springs, ☎ 08-8952 1700 or 1800 896 111; Touring and Information Centre, Ayers Rock Resort, Yulara, ☎ 08-8956 2171.*
● *Sahara Outback Tours, PO Box 3891, Alice Springs, NT 0871, ☎ 08-8953 0881 or 1800 806 240.*

DRIVING TIPS

Most destinations in the Centre are accessible to the family sedan and a 4WD is only necessary for specific destinations. You will, for instance, need a 4WD to visit Finke Gorge National Park, Ruby Gap Nature Park, Rainbow Valley Conservation Area, Chambers Pillar Historical Reserve, Tnorala (Gosse Bluff) Conservation Reserve and the western section of the Simpson Desert Loop.

Distance and fatigue are the driver's greatest enemies in the Territory, so make sure you stop for a break at least every two hours. There is no maximum speed limit in the Territory, but most roads are unfenced and wandering stock is a major hazard. Avoid driving at night, dawn or dusk, when kangaroos and other animals are at their most active and harder to spot. Reduce your speed on unsealed roads, where the stopping distance increases and traction decreases.

When travelling to remote areas, tell a reliable person where you are going and make sure you confirm your arrival to prevent unnecessary searches. Most main roads are sealed and service stations are located every 200–300 km, but plan fuel stops carefully. Always carry sufficient fuel and water, a jack, tow rope, two spare tyres, fan belt, radiator and air-conditioner hoses, a first-aid kit and up-to-date maps. If you're venturing into sandy country, carry sand mats. Lowering tyre pressure or spreading a layer of twigs, leaves or grass can improve traction if you do become bogged.

Treat road trains with great respect. They can be up to three trailers (50 m) long, so give them plenty of room and don't attempt to overtake unless there's at least 1 km of clear road ahead.

Some roads become difficult or impassable after rain. Contact the Northern Territory Department of Transport and Works Road Information Service (☎ 1800 246 199) for a current road report. Don't attempt to cross flooded bridges or causeways unless you are absolutely sure of the water depth. Most flash floods recede within 24 hours. In case of emergency or breakdown, stay with your vehicle. A missing car is easier to spot than a missing person.

COLLECTING FIREWOOD

Remember that it is an offence to collect firewood in national parks and reserves. Fallen timber is home to many plants and animals and helps protect the soil against erosion. If intending to camp in parks and reserves where fires are permitted, make sure you bring your own firewood.

Great care should be taken when overtaking road trains, especially on narrow roads.

VISITING ABORIGINAL COMMUNITIES

Aboriginal people living a semi-traditional life on settlements are shy with strangers. To have a rapport with them requires travelling to their country and, sometimes, paying for the privilege.

Aboriginal territory is privately owned and visitors usually require a written permit. With the exception of the Mereenie Tour Pass, which costs $2.20 and includes an information booklet, all permits are free. Applications should be made in advance of a visit and addressed to the Central Land Council (CLC), 33 Stuart Highway, Alice Springs (☎ 08-8951 6320). Mereenie Tour Passes are also available from the CATIA (☎ 08-8952 5800), Glen Helen Resort (☎ 08-8956 7489), Kings Canyon Resort (☎ 08-8956 7442) and the Ntaria Supermarket in Hermannsburg (☎ 08-8956 7480).

You don't need a permit to travel on public roads within Aboriginal land, but you should refrain from taking sidetracks or going off-road for sightseeing or camping. Some Aboriginal communities, such as Hermannsburg (Ntaria), Wallace Rockhole, Arlparra Store (on the Sandover Highway), Lajamanu, Yuendumu, Yuelamu and Aputula (Finke) allow visitors to enter without a permit to buy food and fuel. Others, such as Docker River, Papunya and Kintore, ask for a transit permit. Check with the CLC before you set out.

Visitors should treat sacred sites with respect and obey entry restrictions.

Transit permits are usually processed within 24 hours of application, but entry permits may take longer to allow time for consultation with Aboriginal landowners. Allow three to four weeks for a reply.

As a result of widespread petrol addiction, AVGAS (aviation fuel) is often the only fuel sold in some remote Western Desert communities. It's best to check ahead on the availability of leaded and unleaded fuel, and to be aware of the possibility of being approached for petrol. Seek local advice on how to deal with these approaches courteously and safely.

Many Aboriginal communities are "dry areas", which means alcohol cannot be taken in or consumed there. Visitors should also ask permission before taking photographs, and respect restrictions.

Essential Information

IN AN EMERGENCY dial 000 for **police**, **fire brigade** *or* **ambulance**.

Alice Springs and Tennant Creek both have **public hospitals** and there are medical centres at Yulara, Hermannsburg (Ntaria) and Oodnadatta.

Police stations are located at the following: Alice Springs, Tennant Creek, Yulara, Kulgera, Kalkaringi, Papunya, Ali Curung, Aputula (Finke), Lajamanu, Ti Tree, Atitjere (Harts Range), Hermannsburg (Ntaria) and Yuendumu.

Business hours are generally Monday–Friday, 9 a.m.–5.30 p.m. although many shops trade later in the evenings and on weekends. In Alice Springs, the Coles supermarket is open 24 hours a day and the Woolworths supermarket is open Monday–Saturday, 7 a.m.–midnight and Sunday 7 a.m.–10 p.m. Markets are held every second Sunday morning in Todd Mall, 9 a.m.–1 p.m. in summer, 9 a.m.–2 p.m. in winter and on Thursday nights from September to December between 6 p.m. and 9 p.m.

All the major Australian **banks** have branches in Alice Springs, with automatic tellers for withdrawals after hours. Banks are

Alice Springs' wide range of shops includes numerous craft centres.

usually open Monday–Thursday, 9.30 a.m.–4 p.m. and Friday 9.30 a.m.–5 p.m. There is a **foreign exchange** booth at Alice Springs airport and in town on Gregory Terrace, near the corner of Todd Street. Some larger hotels also exchange money. The major **credit cards** – American Express, Diners Club, Visa, MasterCard and Bankcard – are accepted by most hotels, restaurants, tour companies, shops and service stations. Most of these businesses also welcome EFTPOS transactions.

Climate: It's unlikely you'll need a raincoat in the Red Centre, which is famed for its clear blue skies. Average maximum daytime temperatures range from 35°C in January to 25°C in June and July, so cool, light clothing is the order of the day. Dress is generally casual, although Lasseters Casino has a "clean, neat and tidy – no work clothes" policy and no "athletic clothes" (tracksuits or sports clothing) after 7 p.m. A hat, water bottle and sunscreen are essential for outdoor pursuits, as are good walking shoes if you intend to take to the tracks. Insect repellent or a fly veil might also come in handy as the Centre's insects can drive people to distraction. Don't forget your swimming costume as the region's waterholes, and the pool at the Alice, provide welcome relief from desert heat. In winter, night-time temperatures can drop as low as 0°C, so pack a jacket, long pants and warm clothes.

Alice Springs has two **newspapers** – the *Centralian Advocate*, published on Tuesday and Friday, and the *Alice Springs News*, available on Wednesdays. **Radio stations** include ABC 783AM, 8HA 900AM, CAAMA Radio 100.7FM, Triple J 94.9FM and Sun-FM 96.9FM. At Yulara, tune in to ABC Regional 99.7FM, ABC Radio National 98.1FM, Triple J 97.5FM or 8HA 900AM. Most of the region's tour companies provide **multilingual guides**, but independent travellers needing the services of German-speaking guides can contact Simone Lienert of Walkabout Australia (☎ 08-8952 2553) or Lilo Raupp of Lilo Guide Service (☎ 08-8952 5079), who can also help you find guides that speak other European languages.

Mobile phone reception via the Telstra network is limited to the immediate area around Alice

Dress codes operate in some establishments, but nightlife is generally informal.

Springs, Yulara (both digital and analogue) and Tennant Creek (digital only). Optus also provides mobile services (digital only) in the Alice Springs area. If you are planning to stay on the highways, there are emergency phones at regular intervals and sufficient traffic not to warrant any extra communications devices.

If, however, you intend to venture off the beaten track, you should consider investing in an EPIRB (Emergency Position Indicating Radio Beacon), costing about $300, which is monitored by satellite and all aircraft. Once activated, it will trigger an immediate search and rescue.

Alternatively, consider hiring a high-frequency (HF) **radio**, which provides emergency access to the Royal Flying Doctor Service (RFDS) in Alice Springs and allows for limited telephone access to pass messages during low traffic periods. The RFDS call sign is VJD and the preferred daytime frequencies are 5410 kHz and 6950 kHz; at night switch to the frequencies 5410 kHz or 2020 kHz.

If you have your own radio, you'll need to obtain a **radio operator's licence** from the Australian Communications Authority (Darwin ☎ 08-8936 3333), then register your licence number and call sign with the RFDS in the Alice (☎ 08-8952 1033). All this will be taken care of if you opt to rent an HF radio from Codan Communications, 1 Hele Crescent, Alice Springs (☎ 08-8955 5455). They charge $75 per week and require a credit-card swipe (refundable) deposit of $500. Codan also hires out satellite phones. Motorola Iridium phones are hand-held but calls are more expensive than calls to and from

Before going bush, let someone know where you are headed and for how long.

NEC Optus Mobilesat vehicle-installed phones. Rental charges are the same for both models – around $900 per month or $250 per week, plus the cost of calls; EPIRBs are also for sale.

Camping equipment can be hired in the Alice from Central Rentals (☎ 08-8952 8077).

Internet and email access is provided by a number of establishments – including the Alice library and airport bistro, Tour Professionals, the Outback Travel Shop, Pioneer Youth Hostel and Melanka Lodge.

Health, hygiene and safety: Sunburn and dehydration are two of the greatest health risks for all travellers in Central Australia. Tap water is generally safe to drink, but outside the main centres water sources may be very limited, so you should always carry your own supplies. If you're planning outdoor activities, take two litres of water for every hour of the activity. If you're travelling to remote areas, allow 10 litres per person for every day of travel to allow for the possibility of breakdown. The incidence of mosquito-borne diseases is much lower in the Red Centre than in the Top End, but use insect repellent for peace of mind and quality sleep.

The Overnight Walkers Registration Scheme is a round-the-clock phone recording service operated by the Parks and Wildlife Commission of the Northern Territory which helps ensure the safety of walkers on designated

The Royal Flying Doctor Service brings health care to remote communities.

tracks in parks and reserves. Visitors planning extended hikes in these areas should ring 1300 650 730 and provide a credit-card number for a $50 per person or $200 group registration fee, which is refunded on deregistration. Alternatively the deposit can be paid in cash at the commission's headquarters, Tom Hare Building, South Stuart Highway, Alice Springs (☎ 08-8951 8211) or the CATIA office at 60 Gregory Terrace, Alice Springs (☎ 08-8952 5199).

Time: The Northern Territory is one hour and 30 minutes ahead of Western Standard Time and half an hour behind Eastern Standard Time. Territorians do not observe daylight saving, but time differences may vary during summer when NSW, Victoria and Tasmania put their clocks forward.

52 THE RED CENTRE

ALICE SPRINGS

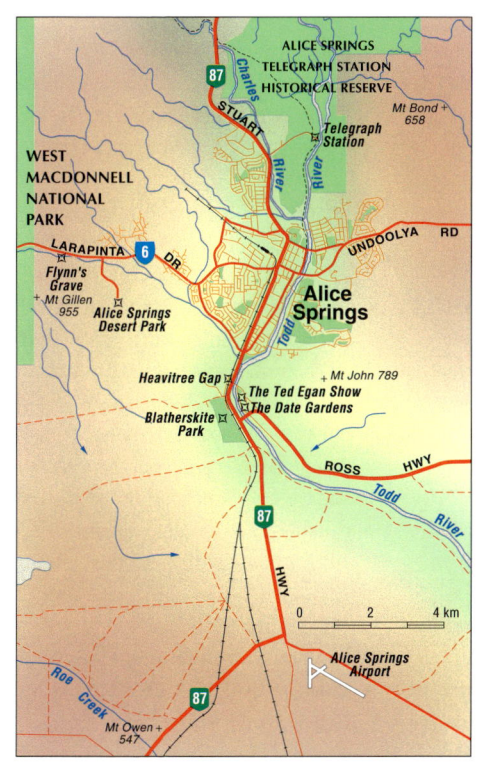

The Telegraph Station borders the spring that gave the Alice its name.

Alice Springs

ALICE SPRINGS FACT FILE

Elevation: 576 m
Population: 25,000–27,000 (subject to seasonal variation)
Location: 1490 km from Darwin, 1530 km from Adelaide and 2958 km from Sydney. There are regular air and bus services, and a train service – The Ghan – from southern cities.
Police: ☎ 08-8951 8888
Fire brigade: ☎ 08-8952 1000
Ambulance: ☎ 08-8952 2200
Hospital: ☎ 08-8951 7777
National road service: ☎ 13 11 11
Local road service: ☎ 08-8952 1087
Visitor Information Centre:
60 Gregory Terrace; open Monday–Friday, 8.30 a.m.–5.30 p.m., weekends and public holidays 9 a.m.–4 p.m. (closed Christmas Day); ☎ 08-8952 5800; fax 08-8953 0295; email: visinfo@catia.asn.au
Transport: the council bus service, Asbus, provides regular services in Alice Springs and its suburbs (☎ 08-8950 0500); Alice Springs Taxis (☎ 13 10 08 or 8952 1877). There are several hire-car companies.

The Alice is a vital service centre for the region's widely scattered population.

Many people returning to Alice Springs after an absence of some years comment that they find it hard to recognise the place. Outback Australia's best-known town is more suburbia-in-the-desert than the dusty watering hole Nevil Shute made famous in his novel *A Town Like Alice*. It wears its modernity well. Originally known as Stuart, its name was changed in 1933 to that of the waterhole named after the wife of Charles Todd, South Australia's Superintendent of Telegraphs. Travellers sampling today's excellent visitor facilities quickly learn to meld a sense of Aboriginal history and European heritage with an appreciation of the haunting landscape.

A short stroll around town provides a wonderful introduction to Red Centre history. Begin at the Visitor Information Centre in Gregory Terrace. Walk to Adelaide House in Todd Mall, then along

Alice Springs 55

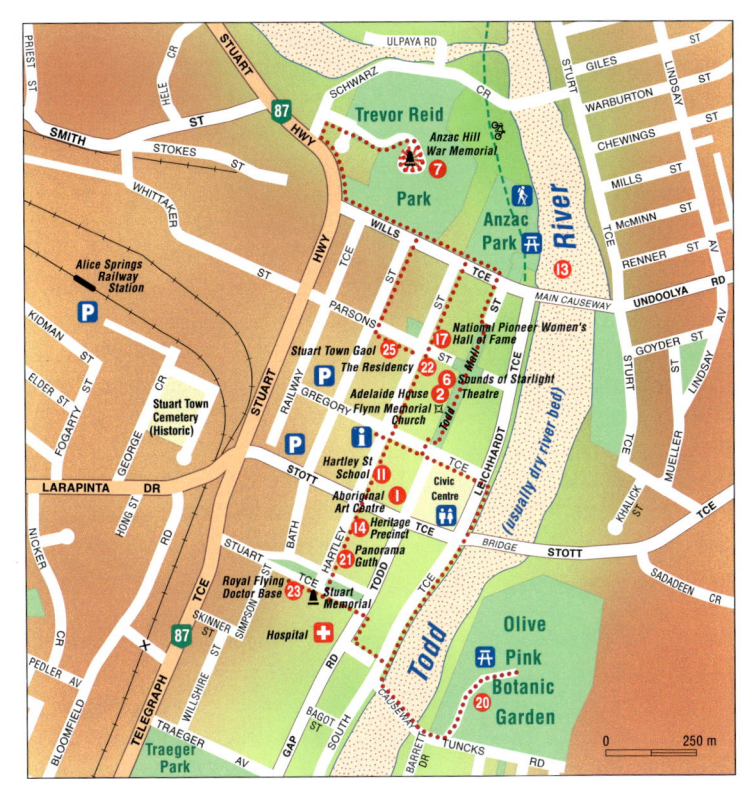

The southern end of the city abuts on the escarpments of the MacDonnell Ranges.

Todd Mall to Anzac Hill for fine views of the town from the summit. Descend to Stuart Town Gaol in Parsons Street. Walk to The Residency and the National Pioneer Women's Hall of Fame at the corner of Parsons and Hartley streets. Continue along Hartley Street to Hartley Street School and Panorama Guth. Proceed through the Heritage Precinct to the RFDS in Stuart Terrace, then head down Stuart Terrace to cross the river by the causeway on Tuncks Road to the Olive Pink Botanic Garden. Picnic here, then return via the Leichhardt Terrace track to the information centre.

Aboriginal Art and Culture Centre ❶

Enrol for an hour in the centre's Didgeridoo University, where the Aboriginal owners guarantee you'll do better than sound like an angry ant. To hear the ancient instrument expertly played, check for one of the performances of song, music and dance. This award-winning centre also features a long-established Aboriginal gallery and organises cultural tours.

86 Todd St. Open daily, 8.30 a.m.–6 p.m. Street parking. Toilets. Wheelchair access. Museum entry, $2; half-day cultural tour: adults, $82.50; children, $44. ☎ 08-8952 3408.

Adelaide House (Frontier Services Museum) ❷

There were no resident doctors when this was Central Australia's only hospital, and nurses had to seek instructions for sometimes complex operations by telegraph. The Reverend John Flynn supervised the design of Adelaide House, which was completed in 1926. Its novel cooling system

Visitors strike up a didgeridoo chorus at the Aboriginal Art and Culture Centre.

BUYING ABORIGINAL ART

Aboriginal art experts advise potential buyers to visit major art galleries and museums in the capital cities to develop an idea of "museum-quality" work. They also recommend reading *Aboriginal Art* by Wally Caruana. Investment buyers should be wary of "tourist-style" works with lots of dots and a "more commercial", brighter colour range. Works by Papunya artists Johnny Warangkula Tjupurrula and Billy Stockman Tjapaltjarri and Utopia artist Emily Kame Kngwarreye have all broken through the $200,000 ceiling. The most sought-after Papunya Tula school paintings are from the beginning of a movement that started when teacher Geoffrey Bardon encouraged the artists to commit their sand paintings to a more permanent surface. Buying directly from a community is wise: it guarantees the artist is adequately paid and the work is authentic, and prices are usually lower. If you can't make it to a community, try the recommended businesses listed in the Reference Directory.

58 THE RED CENTRE

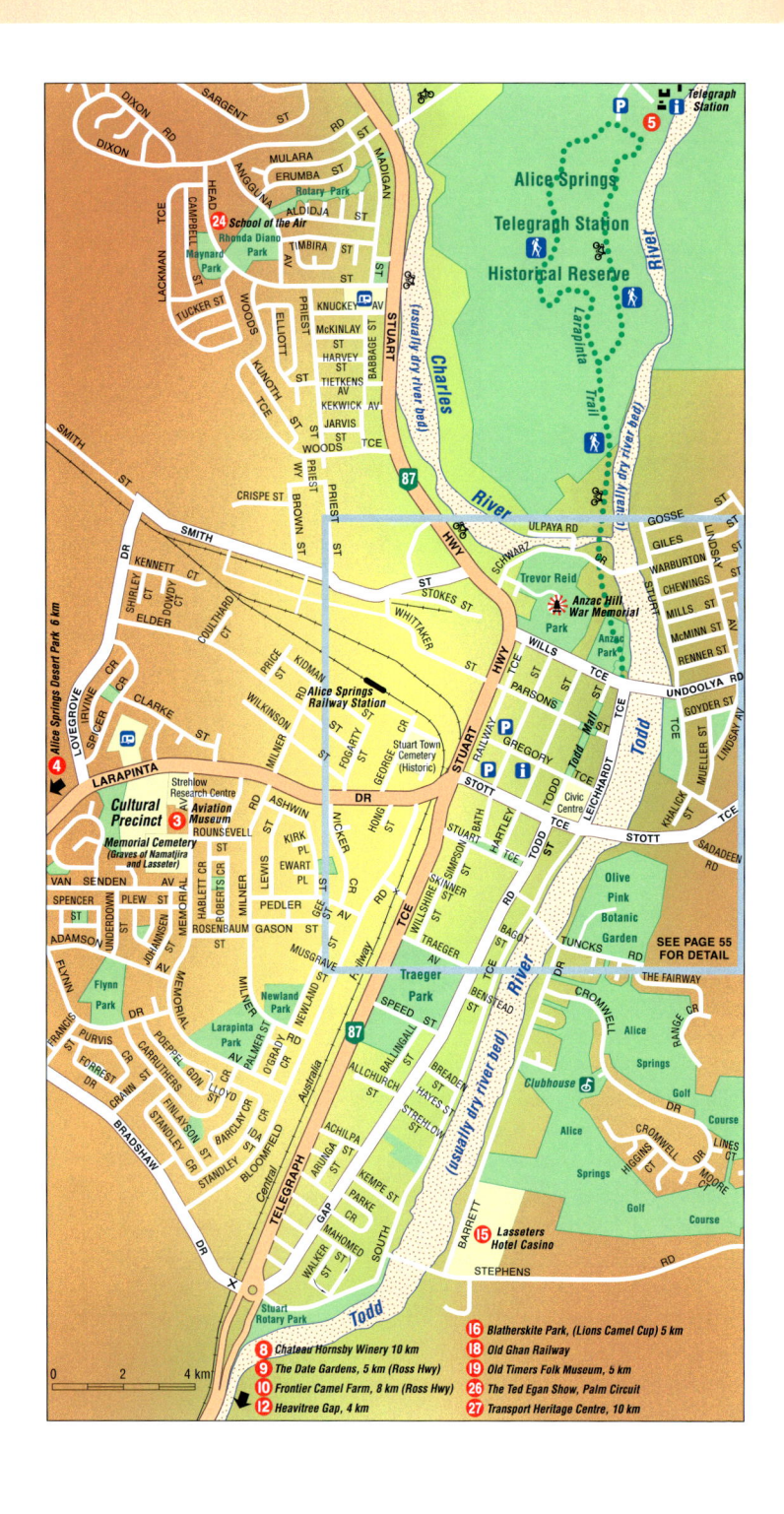

FLYNN OF THE INLAND

The Reverend John Flynn founded the Australian Inland Mission at Oodnadatta in 1911 and was its supervisor for 39 years. By 1918, he had set up hostels and medical services throughout the Australian interior. He began experiments that led to the invention of the pedal radio and supervised the first flight of what was to become the Royal Flying Doctor Service, from Cloncurry, in Queensland, in 1928. John Flynn's Grave Historical Reserve is on Larapinta Drive, 7 km from the Alice.

---

used wet hessian to draw cool air up from the cellar. The building houses the John Flynn Memorial Museum and the John Flynn Memorial Church is next door. At the rear of the house is the small hut where Flynn and Alfred Traeger made radio contact with Hermannsburg in 1926 – Australia's first field radio transmission. Two years later, Traeger invented the pedal radio that was to break the silence of the outback.

48 Todd Mall. Open Monday–Friday, 10 a.m.–4 p.m.; Saturday 10 a.m.–noon. No toilets. Wheelchair access. Adults, $3.30; concession, $2.20; children 12 and under, free. ☎ 08-8952 1856.

Alice Springs Cultural Precinct ❸

An Aboriginal women's Dreaming track runs through what used to be aviator Eddie Connellan's property *Araluen*. Today the area is home to a precinct that brings together several important cultural and historical attractions. **The Araluen Centre for Arts and Entertainment**, noted for its stained-glass windows, has a Sculpture Garden and houses a collection of paintings in the **Albert Namatjira Gallery**. **The Aviation Museum**, in the former Connair hangars, records aviation's dramatic part in the development of the Red Centre. A restored DC3 in Connair livery honours Eddie Connellan's role as founder of the Centre's first airline. As well as a life-saving RFDS aircraft, the museum contains a de Havilland Dove of the Northern Territory Aero Medical Service, which still provides the "mantle of safety" in the north of the Territory.

The Aviation Museum records the contribution aviation has made to the region.

KOOKABURRA

Engine trouble forced pilot Keith Anderson and engineer Bobby Hitchcock to land this monoplane in the Tanami Desert in 1929. They fixed the engine but thick scrub prevented them taking off, and they died of thirst after trying to hack through the bush with a pocketknife. Australian Geographic Society Founder Dick Smith recovered the *Kookaburra* in 1978. It is now in the Aviation Museum.

Aviation's dangers are also made abundantly clear: outside lies the wreck of the *Kookaburra*, while inside is Jim Knight's single-engine Wackett Trainer, which came down on a flight from Melbourne to Perth in 1962. Navigation problems had put Knight so far off course that the aircraft wasn't found for three years – in the Great Victoria Desert in South Australia. Next to the Aviation Museum is the **Memorial Cemetery**, containing the graves of Connellan, Harold Bell Lasseter and indigenous artist Albert Namatjira. There are also the graves of several "Afghan" cameleers, facing in the direction of Mecca, as well as that of anthropologist Olive Pink, facing her beloved Mt Gillen. The natural and cultural history displays at the **Museum of Central Australia** include cosmology and Australian megafauna exhibits.

Cnr Larapinta Dr. and Memorial Ave. Open daily, 10 a.m.–5 p.m. Closed Christmas Day and Good Friday. Parking. Toilets. Wheelchair *access. Admission includes entry to all venues. Adults, $7; concession, $4; family, $18; children under 5, free.* ☎ *08-8951 1120.*

Alice Springs Desert Park

Even if you are short of time, you can still get a feel for the Red Centre's habitats and sight a numbat or a mala at this display of desert diversity in the foothills of the MacDonnell Ranges. If you have some extensive travel in mind, treat it as an essential preview and take a close look at some of the plants and endangered animals you're unlikely to come across in the field. The 1300 ha Desert Park, which includes a fine nocturnal house and aquarium, debunks the belief that deserts are lifeless wastelands. With 350 plant species and 120 animal species – 11 of them threatened or endangered – from the Centre, the park stresses the interaction of plants, animals and people, and explores the region's main environments. It has more than 26 major features, including a free-flying birds of prey display, and 6 km of walking tracks, so allow at least 3 hours.

On Larapinta Drive, 6 km west of the Alice. Open daily, 7.30 a.m.– 6 p.m., last entry 5 p.m. Closed Christmas Day. Parking. Toilets. BBQ and picnic area. Wheelchair access. Gift shop. Cafe. Function area. Adults, $18; concession, $9. ☎ *08-8951 8788.*

For guaranteed sightings of local flora and fauna, visit Alice Springs Desert Park.

The manicured lawns of the Telegraph Station make a great spot for a picnic.

Alice Springs Telegraph Station Historical Reserve ❺

Try the corned-beef rolls or hot soup and damper cooked on the original stove of a kitchen that was part of the first European settlement in Alice Springs. Built in 1872 to relay messages by the Overland Telegraph between Adelaide and Darwin, the Telegraph Station operated for 60 years. It also housed the first police station in Central Australia. In 1932, it became a school for Aboriginal children, and in 1963 it was declared a Historic Reserve. The attractive stone buildings have been restored and the reserve is a lovely place to walk or picnic. It's even possible to cool off in the waterhole that gave the town its name.

Stuart Hwy, 4 km north of town centre. Reserve open daily, May–September, 8 a.m.–7 p.m.; October–April, 8 a.m.–9 p.m. Historical precinct open daily, 8 a.m.–5 p.m. Parking. Toilets. Wheelchair access. No charge for entry to the reserve. Historical precinct entry – adults, $6; concession, $4.50; children under 14, $3. Cafe. Picnic tables. BBQ. ☎ 08-8952 3993.

Andrew Langford's Sounds of Starlight Theatre ❻

In this popular, interactive show Andrew Langford demonstrates the didgeridoo skills he learnt while living with Aboriginal people. The show also features photographic slides and special effects celebrating the history of Central Australia.

40 Todd Mall. Open April–November, Tuesday–Saturday, 7.30 p.m.–8.20 p.m., bookings recommended. Parking at rear. Toilets. Wheelchair access if booked. Adults, $16.50; concession, $12; children, $11; family, $44. ☎ 08-8953 0826.

Anzac Hill ❼

The view of the MacDonnell Ranges at dawn and dusk from what Aboriginals call Untyeye Artwilye is one of Alice's best-kept secrets. Emily and Heavitree gaps, the Todd River and Billy Goat Hill, at the other end of town – all important in Dreamtime lore – are visible from here. There is a drive or walk to the top.

No toilets. Limited wheelchair access.

Chateau Hornsby Winery ❽

People sometimes refuse to believe there is a winery in Alice Springs, but they're soon convinced when they learn it's had a very Red Centre problem with termites in the vines. As well as growing classic grape varieties like riesling,

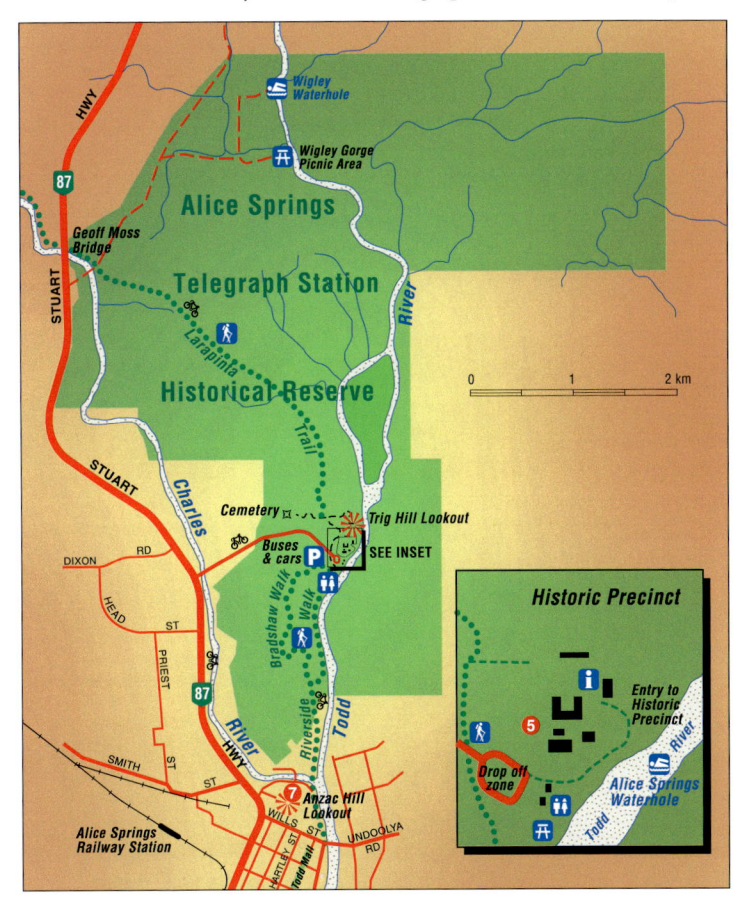

Visitors enjoy a picnic in the shade of the Date Garden's century-old palms.

Chateau Hornsby, the Centre's only winery, produces wine from five grape varieties.

shiraz and cabernet sauvignon, pharmacist Denis Hornsby has made this a major entertainment and function centre, complete with an underground winery. Guests on New Year's Eve go into the vineyard to pick grapes for what Denis claims is the world's first vintage of the new year.

Petrick Rd, about 10 km southeast of town centre. Open daily, 9 a.m.–5 p.m. Closed December and January. Sunday jazz. Parking. Toilets. Wheelchair access. Bush restaurant. ☎ *08-8955 5133.*

The Date Gardens ⑨

Transplanted from their original sites around Alice Springs, many of the palms in The Date Gardens are between 80 and 100 years old. Enjoy their shade, savour their fruit and learn more about what may be the oldest cultivated crop in the world. You can even take a camel to dinner from here (see Frontier Camel Farm, below).

On Ross Hwy, 5 km south of town centre. Open daily, 9 a.m.–6 p.m. Closed from Christmas until New Year. Parking. Toilets. Wheelchair access. Cafe/evening bush restaurant (bookings only). Entertainment Monday, Wednesday and Friday evenings; bookings essential. Picnic tables. BBQ. ☎ *08-8952 8493.*

Frontier Camel Farm ⑩

Drop in to get a feel for the days when camels were the 4WDs of the outback. Take a camel to breakfast through the soft morning light (adults, $55; concession, $35) or to dinner at The Date Gardens ($85; $65) or go on a camel ramble along the Todd River ($45; $25). The Arid Australia Reptile Display and Camel Museum explain the story of camels in Australia and the legendary "Ghans".

Ross Hwy, about 8 km south-east of town centre. Open daily except Christmas, New Year's Day and during the Camel Cup (July), 9 a.m.–5 p.m. Parking. Toilets. Wheelchair access. Adults, $10; concession, $9; family, $25 (all include short camel ride); family (entry only), $12. Cafe. Picnic tables.
☎ *08-8953 0444.*

Hartley Street School ⓫

Sit in a classroom of Alice's historic school, which opened in 1930 with two rooms and one teacher. It closed in 1965 and is now the local office of the National Trust. This is where you can find plenty of information about the Alice Springs of old and pick up a range of specialist publications on the subject. A small area has been set up as a traditional schoolroom.

Hartley St. Open Monday–Friday, 10.30 a.m.–2.30 p.m. Closed public holidays. Street parking. No toilets. Wheelchair access.
☎ *08-8952 4516.*

Heavitree Gap ⓬

Most visitors to Alice Springs come from the south. Passing through this majestic gateway (known to the Arrernte as Ntaripe), where the Todd River cuts through the MacDonnell Ranges, means that they have reached their destination.

Stuart Hwy, about 4 km south of town centre.

Henley-on-Todd Regatta ⓭

See the sand fly at the biggest event on the Alice Springs calendar. On the last Saturday in September or the first in October, the dry riverbed of the Todd "launches" a flotilla of bottomless race boats. Lifesavers look on, ready to rescue competitors in

The Henley-on-Todd Regatta is one boat race that holds no fears for nonswimmers.

Jockeys steer their charges towards the finishing line during the Lions Camel Cup.

danger of drowning in the sand. Rotarians first staged the event in 1961 and have since used it to raise more than $1 million for community projects. In 1993 disaster struck – the river filled and the regatta had to be cancelled.

Todd River, near Wills Tce. Parade through town 11 a.m.; events on river begin noon. Parking. Toilets. Wheelchair access. Adults, $10; concession, $5; family, $20; children under 15, $5; children under 5, free. Bar/food stalls. No picnic tables or BBQ. ☎ *08-8955 1253.*

Heritage Precinct ⓴

This area contains buildings constructed in the 1930s and '40s that demonstrate architectural solutions to life in the arid Centre.

Stott Tce, near Hartley St, and extending south to hospital.

Lasseters Hotel Casino ⓯

Offers all the gambling, dining, entertainment and accommodation facilities of a modern casino but with the advantage of being set against the backdrop of the ancient MacDonnell Ranges.

93 Barrett Dr. Casino open daily, 10 a.m.–3 a.m. (till 4 a.m. Friday and Saturday); Limerick Inn open daily, 4 p.m.–late. Parking. Toilets. Wheelchair access. Restaurant. ☎ *08-8950 7777 or 1800 808 975.*

Lions Camel Cup ⓰

Camels, they say, have minds of their own. Discover for yourself just what erratic racers they are at this hilarious event, normally held by the local Lions clubs in July. A grand parade gets things underway and is followed by races throughout the afternoon, as well

OLIVE PINK

Miss Olive Pink's notoriety often overshadows her hard-earned reputation as an anthropologist. Arriving in Central Australia in 1930, she lived for many years among the Aboriginal people of the Tanami Desert and was ever after an ardent advocate of Aboriginal rights. In 1956, she became honorary curator of the flora reserve she had campaigned hard to establish. Pink ran it almost as a fortress, and visitors had to be invited in. She named trees after prominent public figures and if the identities did not perform to her high standards the trees would not be watered. The reserve was given her name after she died in 1975, aged 91. She is buried in the Memorial Cemetery, where, passionate till the end, hers is the only grave facing west. It is said she wanted to see the sun set over Mt Gillen.

as some novelty events. The day ends with a game of pocamelo – polo on camels – at about 5 p.m.

Blatherskite Park, on Stuart Hwy, about 5 km south of town centre. Starts 10.30 a.m. Parking and free bus to and from town. Toilets. Wheelchair access. Adults, $8; children, $4. Bar/food stalls. No BBQ or picnic tables. ☎ 08-8953 2300.

National Pioneer Women's Hall of Fame (at the Old Courthouse) ⑰

From the first women to graduate from Australian universities in the 1880s to the first women ordained as priests in the 1990s, this national project celebrates the role of women in Australia's heritage and describes some of the obstacles they have overcome. The project was founded by Molly Clark, of Old Andado station. The heritage-listed Old Courthouse, built in 1928, also contains displays of early domestic equipment.

Cnr Hartley and Parsons sts. Open daily, 10 a.m.–5 p.m. and by appointment. Closed mid-December until early February. No parking. No toilets. Wheelchair access. Adults, $2.20; children, free. Souvenir shop. ☎ 08-8952 9006.

Old Ghan Railway ⑱

Step back in time to 1929, when the railway line finally reached Alice Springs and The Ghan train provided the first public transport to the Centre. The Old Ghan Train runs on a restored section of its original narrow-gauge track, departing from MacDonnell Siding, a 1930s-style railway station built from plans originally intended for Stuart (Alice Springs) (see Transport Heritage Centre, p. 73).

Old Timers Folk Museum [19]

A folk history of early European settlement is told here, with photographic and other material drawn from the families of pioneers. Because much of Central Australia's European story is so recent, it is still possible to bump into some of those enterprising souls, now resident in the nursing home/retirement village where the museum is situated.

In Old Timers Village, on Stuart Hwy, 5 km south of town centre. Open daily, 2 p.m.–4 p.m. Closed November–March. Parking. Toilets. Wheelchair access. Adults, $2; children, free. Souvenir shop. ☎ 08-8952 2844, ext. 255.

Olive Pink Botanic Garden [20]

Sponsor your own "family tree" here in the botanic gardens of Central Australia. More than 300 different species of Central Australian plants are displayed in a variety of desert settings. All are labelled and signs throughout the garden provide information on plant distribution, habitat and Aboriginal uses, but they vie for attention with the views from Meyers Hill, a registered Aboriginal sacred site that dominates the garden. In the visitor centre, displays explain the evolution of Australia's arid-zone flora.

Tuncks Rd, on the eastern side of Todd River, about 1.5 km from town centre. Gardens open daily, 10 a.m.–6 p.m.; visitor centre open daily, 10 a.m.–4 p.m. Both closed Christmas Day and Good Friday. Parking. Toilets. Wheelchair access (except hill walk). Entry by donation. Picnic tables. ☎ 08-8952 2154.

The famous Ghan train is run and maintained by a band of dedicated volunteers.

Guides at the Royal Flying Doctor Visitor Centre explain the service's crucial role.

Panorama Guth ㉑

Henk Guth's 360-degree painting stands 6 m high and is 60 m in circumference. Painted with the help of another Dutch artist in 1975, it shows the major landmarks of the Red Centre. The gallery contains paintings by Henk and others and an intriguing collection of Aboriginal artefacts.

65 Hartley St. Open Monday–Saturday, 9 a.m.–5 p.m.; Sunday and public holidays, noon–5 p.m. except December, January and February. Street parking. Toilets. Limited wheelchair access. Adults, $5.50; children, $3.30. ☎ 08-8952 2013.

The Residency ㉒

Most visitors to this splendid building ask to see the bathroom Queen Elizabeth II used when she visited in 1963, earning The Residency the nickname "Palace in the Alice". Alas, it is no more, having been removed to create office space. Built in 1927 as the home of Central Australia's regional administrator, The Residency has been restored in the style of that period. Its furnishings provide fascinating insights into the European history of the Centre.

Cnr Parsons and Hartley sts. Open Monday–Friday, 9 a.m.–5 p.m.; weekends 10 a.m.–5 p.m. Closed Christmas Day and Good Friday. No parking. No toilets. Wheelchair access. No admission charge. ☎ 08-8951 5688.

Royal Flying Doctor Visitor Centre ㉓

This base is just as important today as when it was established in 1939. The Royal Flying Doctor Service (RFDS) still provides the "mantle of safety" envisaged by its founder, the Reverend John Flynn, for people living in outback towns, communities and stations. You can join a tour to learn about today's operations as well as the equipment and services of the past. Then relax and enjoy morning or afternoon tea in one of the town's finest heritage buildings.

Stuart Tce. Open Monday–Saturday, 9 a.m.–4 p.m. (last tour begins); Sunday and public holidays, 1 p.m.–4 p.m. (last tour). Tours begin on the hour and half-hour. Parking. Toilets. Wheelchair access. Adults, $5.25; students, $3.15; children, $2.10. Cafe/souvenir shop. ☎ *08-8952 1129.*

School of the Air ㉔

To be sure of seeing and hearing teachers giving lessons to children as far as 1000 km away, visit during weekday mornings. Afternoon transmissions are less frequent and sometimes break up. But don't despair if you can't make it then; a video shows how the school works, and you can hear audio recordings of typical lessons at other times.

Head St, 2.5 km north of town. Visitor centre open Monday–Saturday, 8.30 a.m.–4.30 p.m.; Sunday 1.30 p.m.–4.30 p.m. Closed Christmas, Boxing and New Year's days and Good Friday. Limited off-street parking. Toilets. Wheelchair access. Adults, $3.50; senior concession and children, $2.50; family, $12. ☎ *08-8951 6834.*

Stuart Town Gaol ㉕

Petty criminals, and some not so petty who were later sent to jails or even execution in the south, were housed in this no-frills building built in 1907–08. Prior to its

The elegant interior of The Residency has been lovingly restored in 1920s style.

official opening in 1909, prisoners had been held at Heavitree Gap. Now run by the National Trust, it has two cells once used to segregate Aboriginal and European prisoners, and an exercise yard at the back.

8 Parsons St. Open Monday–Friday, 10 a.m.–12.30 p.m.; Saturday, 9.30 a.m.–noon. Closed public holidays. No parking. No toilets. Adults, $2.20; National Trust members and children, free. ☎ 08-8952 4516.

Ted Egan Show ㉖

Poet, historian and storyteller Ted Egan is one of the area's characters. He entertains visitors with songs, such as his well-known *Drover's Boy*, and stories collected during almost five decades spent in the Northern Territory. He provides his own musical accompaniment by tapping out tunes on the beer-carton instrument he invented.

At the Settlers Function Rooms, Palm Circuit. Performances April–October, Monday–Thursday, 8 p.m.

SCHOOL OF THE AIR

The Galah sessions on the School of the Air were the day's highlight for many pupils, when children living hundreds of kilometres apart could swap stories about their families, pets and remote lives. Some schools even had choirs whose singers had never met. The School of the Air remains an important institution in the outback and Alice's, which opened in 1951 using the two-way radio network of the RFDS, was Australia's first. Former pupils still tell stories of classes being interrupted by medical emergencies such as a ringer being gored by a bull or the camp cook being bitten by a mulga snake.

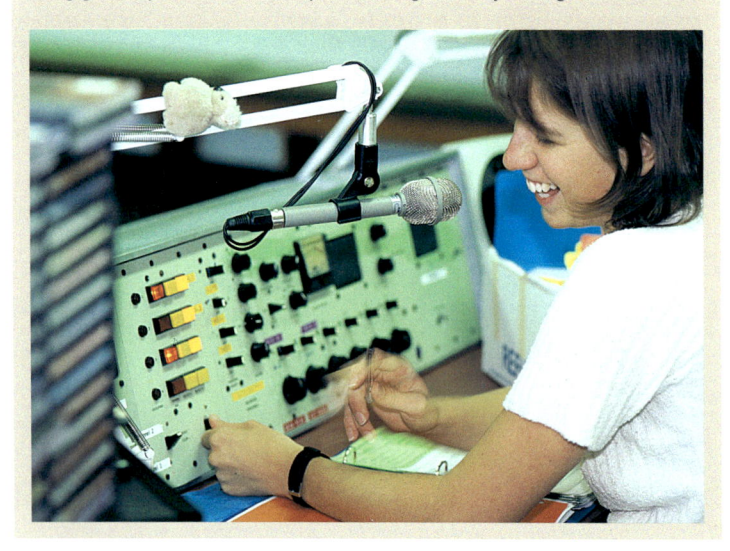

Alice Springs 73

Viewing vintage vehicles inspires admiration for the Red Centre's transport pioneers.

Wheelchair access. Adults, $15; students to 18 years, $10; children under 10, free. Dinner is available before the show at 6.30 p.m.
☎ *08-8952 9952.*

Transport Heritage Centre ㉗

The centre incorporates the Old Ghan Train and the Road Transport Hall of Fame. Transport and communications have always presented major challenges in the outback, and the centre's displays explain how inhabitants dealt with them. Ride in the Old Ghan on its original narrow-gauge track (a vintage NSU diesel locomotive departs MacDonnell Siding on Wednesdays, Fridays and Sundays at 10 a.m. for a 90-minute return trip to Mount Ertiva, about 8 km away). On two Sundays a month, a W-class steam loco takes the train on a five-hour, 25 km journey to Ewaninga. The Road Transport Hall of Fame features a 1934 AEC truck said to be Australia's first road train – they now carry most of the region's freight – as well as other vintage vehicles.

MacDonnell Siding, Norris Bell Ave, 10 km south of town. Open daily, 9 a.m.–5 p.m. Train closed Christmas public holidays (sometimes others); Hall of Fame closed Christmas Day and Good Friday. Parking. Toilets. Wheelchair access. Hall of Fame – adults, $5; concession, $4; children, $2.50; family, $12. Old Ghan Train – adults, $5; concession, $4; children, $3; family, $12. Return train ride to Mount Ertiva – adults, $15; concession, $13; children, $9, under 6, free. Return train ride to Ewaninga (including lunch) – adults, $30; concession, $26; children, $20; under 6, free. Cafe at train station; kiosk in Hall of Fame. Train ☎ *08-8955 5047; Hall of Fame* ☎ *08-8952 7161.*

74 THE RED CENTRE

WEST OF ALICE SPRINGS

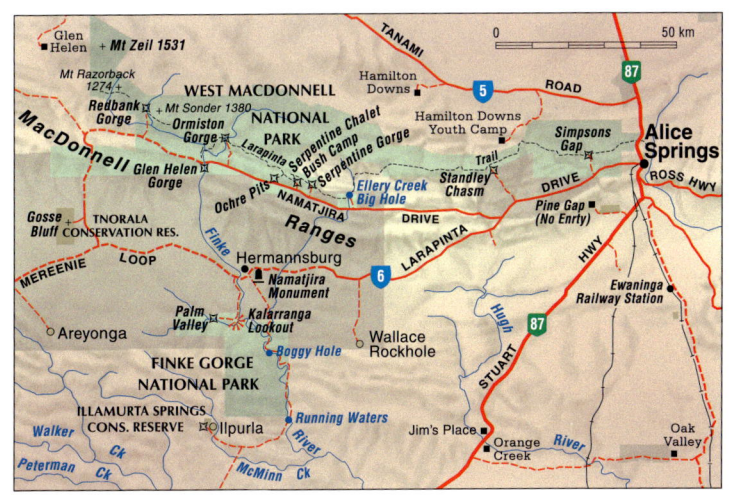

Gosse Bluff Meteor Crater rises abruptly from the plain south of Tyler Pass.

West of Alice Springs

It's hard to imagine a greater paradox than the region west of Alice Springs. At first glance it's rugged, inhospitable territory, awesome in its isolation, breathtaking in its ferocious orange beauty. The cliffs and gorges beckon with an edge of danger and the views are sensational, but care should be taken as many of the clifftops are unfenced and can be crumbly. Yet closer inspection of this harsh landscape reveals an environment teeming with life – from the mouse-sized, fat-tailed antechinus to fleet-footed rock-wallabies, mighty river red gums to delicate Centralian flannel

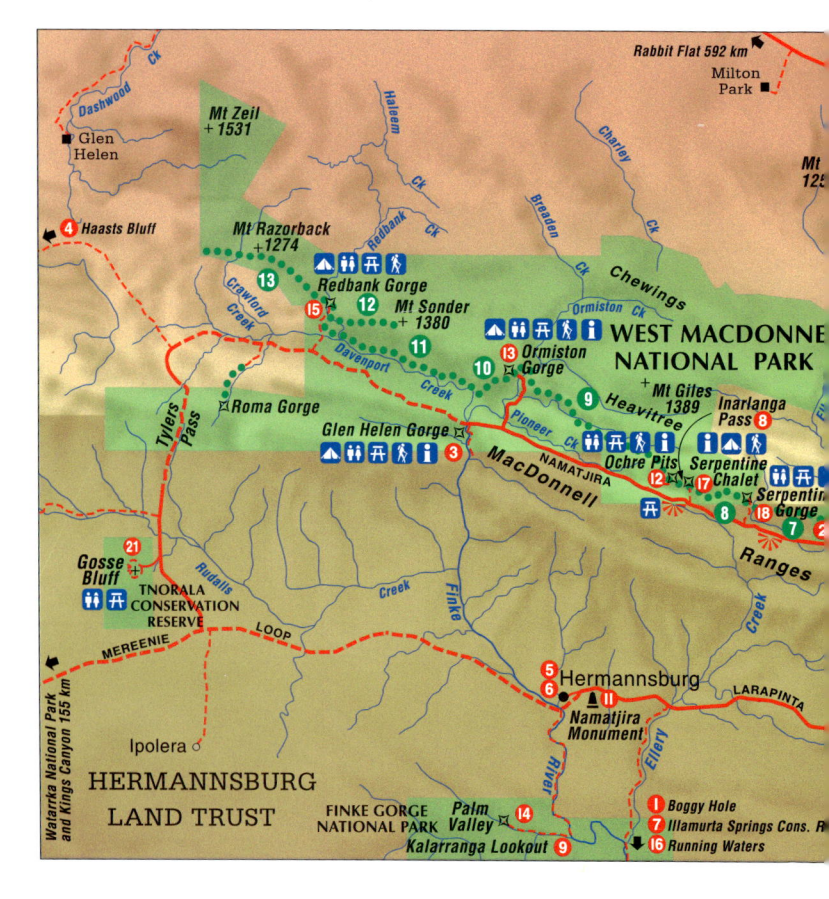

West of Alice Springs

flowers. The gaping slashes through the ragged ridges of the West MacDonnell Ranges closet waterholes and provide shade and sanctuary for myriad plants and animals. During the midday heat they are also a refuge for visitors exploring the West MacDonnell National Park.

During his three attempts to cross the continent from south to north between 1860 and 1862, John MacDouall Stuart named the MacDonnell Ranges for the South Australian governor of the time, Sir Richard MacDonnell.

> An Aboriginal Dreaming tells of a group of young spirit ancestors who were burned in a bushfire. They were picked up by a gale, and with their bodies still alight, dropped in the Finke Gorge area, where they became palms and cycads. The shaggy leaves represent the ancestors' traditional headdresses and the dark trunks their fire-blackened bodies.

The quartzite ridges of the MacDonnell Ranges stretch 160 km west of Alice Springs.

The western side of these ranges forms the backbone of the region affectionately known as the West Macs. Its other outstanding feature is the Finke River, the main artery of Central Australia, also named by Stuart in honour of his friend and financier, South Australian pastoralist William Finke. From its source in the West MacDonnells, this mighty watercourse wends its way for 690 km across the arid plains to the western edge of the Simpson Desert.

The combination of rugged ranges and an ancient river and its tributaries means that most of the attractions in the West Macs are natural. Many are accessible from the sealed Larapinta and Namatjira drives on a day trip from the Alice.

NATIONAL PARKS

West MacDonnell National Park occupies a vast area of more than 1330 sq. km along the West MacDonnell Ranges. It extends more than 160 km from the outskirts of Alice Springs west to the Territory's highest peak, Mt Zeil. The mountains rise like islands from the flat Central Australian desert plains and are punctuated by spectacular gorges, rocky ridges and tranquil, river red gum-lined waterholes. Highlights include Simpsons Gap, Ormiston Gorge and Pound, and Glen Helen and Redbank gorges. Most can be visited in 2WD vehicles on a day trip from Alice Springs.

Visitors with more time can take in some great bushwalking

that ranges from short half-hour nature tracks to more challenging overnight walks. The park is home to the Western Arrernte people and contains many places of spiritual significance to them. They are consulted on its management and the presentation of information on their culture. (See p. 181 in the Reference Directory for Aboriginal culture tours.) The main roads through the park are Namatjira Drive and Larapinta Drive. The latter also provides access to the Aboriginal communities of Hermannsburg (Ntaria) and Wallace Rockhole.

There are no entry fees to the park, though campers will be charged $5 or $2.50 per night depending on the level of facilities. Bush campers and overnight walkers must obtain a $2.50 per adult per night permit from ranger stations or the PWC of the NT (☎ 08-8951 8211). Ranger stations are located at Simpsons Gap (☎ 08-8955 0310) and Ormiston Gorge (☎ 08-8956 7799).

Drive through in a coach or car if time is limited, but for an in-depth encounter with the ancient landscape of the West MacDonnell Ranges it's hard to beat a trek on the long-distance walking track known as the **Larapinta Trail**, which when completed will wind about 250 km from Alice Springs to Mt Sonder. The track is designed for capable bushwalkers who are prepared to carry reasonable loads and camp out, but walkers can join or leave it at a number of access points along the way, choosing to complete anything from an easy day-hike to a week-long trek. For those with limited bush experience, Section 1 (23.7 km) linking the Alice Springs Overland Telegraph Station with Simpsons Gap is

> I was literally surrounded by fair flowers of many a changing hue ... They alone would have induced me to name this Glen Flora; but having found in it also so many of the stately palm trees, I have called it the Glen of Palms.
> —Explorer Ernest Giles, on recording the cabbage palms along the Finke River in 1872

Even novice bushwalkers can hike parts of the long-distance Larapinta Trail.

ideal. There are basic camping facilities (water, toilets and gas barbecues) near Wallaby Gap 13.4 km from the station. The first section passes poles of the now-abandoned Overland Telegraph Line and provides splendid views of Alice Springs and Mt Gillen. Section 3 from Jay Creek to Standley Chasm (14 km) is a much more arduous trek through mountainous terrain, suitable only for experienced and well-prepared walkers. The PWC has produced a series of brochures on each section, available from their headquarters at the Arid Zone Research Institute on the South Stuart Highway, 10 km from Alice Springs (☎ 08-8951 8211). Walkers are strongly advised to participate in the Overnight Walker Registration Scheme (☎ 1300 650 730; see Essential Information, p. 48). Several tour operators provide supported walking tours on the track (see Reference Directory).

Finke Gorge National Park is an area of 46,000 ha about 140 km south-west of Alice Springs. The park is home to more than 400 plant species, some 30 of them rare or relict, including about 1800 mature red cabbage palms that are unique to the area. They survive thanks to the shady gorges that preserve moisture in this otherwise arid zone. Accessible only by high-clearance 4WD, the park nonetheless receives 80,000 visitors annually. Palm Valley and Boggy Hole are popular camping and bushwalking destinations.

One of the Finke's few permanent waterholes, Boggy Hole is a popular camping spot.

Despite its erratic flow, the Finke sustains mammals, birds and nine species of fish.

Although both sites are located within the park, there is no direct access from Palm Valley to Boggy Hole as the Finke riverbed is too sandy to cross. Visitors must backtrack from Palm Valley via Hermannsburg to the Finke River 4WD Route that follows the riverbed beyond the park, and goes through Running Waters and Illamurta Conservation Reserve on its way to Watarrka National Park. No entry fees apply, though Palm Valley campers are charged $5 per adult. The ranger station is at Palm Valley (☎ 08-8956 7401).

Boggy Hole ❶
A police camp was established here on the Finke River in 1889 in an attempt to crush Aboriginal resistance to pastoral settlement. It was closed after officer-in-charge William Henry Wiltshire was charged with, though later acquitted of, murdering six Aboriginal people. Today the waterhole is an important habitat for fish and

FINKE RIVER

Lherepirnte, the Western Arrernte name for the Finke River, means salty river – a reference to the brackish nature of the water in some of the river's downstream pools during dry periods. The name, anglicised as Larapinta, has been given to the region's major walking track (see Larapinta Trail, p. 79) and to one of the main access roads into the West MacDonnell Ranges. Along with the Hugh River and Ellery Creek, which form part of the Finke's 38,000 sq. km catchment area, the river has followed approximately the same course for at least 100 million years – perhaps as long as 250 million. When the Finke was establishing its path, Australia was still part of the supercontinent Gondwana, the first mammals and flowers were evolving on land, and dinosaurs were becoming extinct.

The parched course of the Finke emerges from the MacDonnells at Glen Helen Gorge.

waterbirds and a popular camping ground and swimming spot among 4WD enthusiasts.

On Finke River, 32 km south of Hermannsburg. Open continuously. Parking. No toilets. Camping. Bring your own firewood.

Ellery Creek Big Hole ❷

The dramatic rock walls on either side of Ellery Creek provide a graphic timeline of Central Australia's geological history from 850 to 310 million years ago. The 3 km Dolomite Walk loop explains how folding and faulting have revealed chapters in the land's past. Visitors can cool off under the big river red gums and take a dip in the Big Hole, but should be wary of submerged rocks and logs, and carry an air mattress as the water can be extremely cold.

Off Namatjira Dr, 90 km from the Alice. Open continuously. Parking. Toilets. Picnic tables. BBQ. Camping, caravans permitted. Bring your own firewood.

Glen Helen Gorge ❸

The permanent waterhole at the entrance to Glen Helen Gorge is a dry-season refuge for all nine species of fish found in the Finke River, as well as waterbirds including the Pacific heron, grey teal, swan and a variety of waders. Occasionally, an osprey or an Australian crake also uses the waterhole as a pit stop during migration. Visitors can gain a bird's-eye view of the gorge, which has been slowly carved by the Finke River through the Pacoota sandstone over at least 100 million years, by taking a helicopter flight from the resort in the former Glen Helen station homestead. Tours of the area by motorbike can be arranged from Alice Springs. To further explore the gorge, and to see the Organ Pipes rock formation, swim across the waterhole or, when the water is low enough, climb over the ridge to reach the southern side. Glen Helen Gorge is called Yaperlpe by the Western Arrernte, who believe it is guarded by an ancestral carpet snake.

Off Namatjira Dr, 135 km west of Alice. Open continuously. Parking. Toilets. Restaurant/bar. Picnic tables. Store/fuel. Resort and budget accommodation/camping, caravans permitted. Resort ☎ 08-8956 7489.

Haasts Bluff ❹

While no permits are required to travel the 4WD-only Haasts Bluff Road connecting the Tanami Road and Namatjira Drive, the route does cross Aboriginal land and travellers are not allowed to venture more than 50 m from the roadside. From the road, they can, however, obtain a clear view of the sheer quartzite walls of Haasts Bluff, which also gives its name to a nearby Aboriginal community. A permit from the Central Land Council is required to visit the community, which is home to an important emerging art group – the Ikuntji Women's Centre.

Albert Namatjira, painted by William Dargie, 1956. Queensland Art Gallery.

HERMANNSBURG (NTARIA) FACT FILE

Elevation: 550 m
Population: fluctuates around 500
Location: 125 km south-west of Alice Springs, about one hour and 30 minutes drive from Alice Springs.
Police: ☎ 08-8956 7422
Clinic: ☎ 08-8956 7433
National road service: ☎ 13 11 11
Tourist information: ☎ 08-8956 7402 (see Hermannsburg Historic Precinct opening hours).
Ntaria Supermarket (☎ 08-8956 7480) sells groceries, takeaways and fuel; no EFTPOS available.
No accommodation. Nearest camping is at Palm Valley, 20 km away and accessible only by high-clearance 4WD, or Wallace Rockhole, 51 km distant.

Hermannsburg (Ntaria)

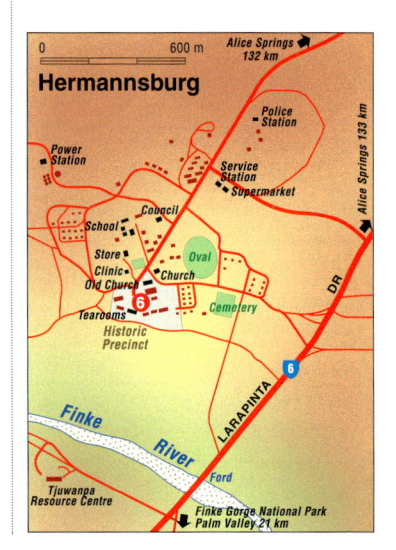

Whitewashed buildings and picket fences are more suggestive of a 19th century German farming village than the contemporary Aboriginal community that is Hermannsburg (Ntaria) today. The neatly preserved buildings are the remnants of a mission established by the Lutheran Church in 1877. Although the mission was phased out and the land handed back to its traditional owners in 1982, many of the buildings are preserved in a historic precinct. Anthropologist Ted Strehlow, a son of one of the early missionaries, spent his formative years here and later devoted his life to chronicling Arrernte life and culture. Aboriginal artist Albert Namatjira was born at the mission and raised his family of 10 children here. Hermannsburg still has a thriving arts community and paintings, pottery and silk-screens are for sale at the Kata Anga Tearoom in the Historic Precinct and at galleries in Alice Springs. Note that Hermannsburg is an alcohol-free community and penalties apply for not complying with the prohibition.

Hermannsburg Historic Precinct ❻

Two Namatjira watercolours are the prize exhibits in the gallery in the historic precinct, where a number of buildings from the days of the former Lutheran mission are preserved. Namatjira prints and works by local artists and potters are sold at the Kata Anga Tearoom, which serves morning and afternoon teas and light lunches to raise funds for future conservation and restoration.

Off Larapinta Dr, 125 km west of Alice. Open daily except Christmas Day–New Year's Day and Good Friday, March to November, 9 a.m.– 4 p.m., December to February, 10 a.m.–4 p.m. Parking. Toilets. Wheelchair access. Adults, $4.50, $3.50 extra for art gallery; children, $3, $3 extra for art gallery; family, $12, $12 extra for art gallery. Cafe. Picnic tables. ☎ *08-8956 7402.*

Illamurta Springs Conservation Reserve ❼

In the late 19th century, a police camp was sited on this permanent spring in an attempt to stop Aboriginals from killing pastoralists' cattle. It opened in 1893, after the closure of the short-lived police station at Boggy Hole, and

The perceptions of a lifetime thus confirm the impressions of the few white artists who have painted in that country and who scarcely dared to show the result because of its unbelievable richness of colour.
—Namatjira catalogue, 1938

ALBERT NAMATJIRA

Albert Namatjira's watercolours provided many Australians with their introduction to the vivid landscape of the Red Centre. Born at Hermannsburg in 1902, Namatjira attended the mission school but was also initiated into tribal life. He received his first art lessons from visiting artist Rex Battarbee in 1934 and held his first exhibition in Melbourne four years later. It sold out in two days. Namatjira died in 1959. His grave at the Memorial Cemetery in Alice Springs is marked by a beautiful headstone.

The Mpaara Track traverses the smooth sandstone cliffs near Kalarranga Lookout.

continued to operate as an administrative centre and distribution point for rations for dispossessed Aboriginal people until 1912. Today, all that remains are camp ruins and the spring itself, which attracts birds and provides a habitat for several relict plant species. This site forms part of the Python Dreaming and a large number of stone artefacts provide evidence of Aboriginal occupation.

225 km south-west of the Alice via Ernest Giles Rd, 28 km west of Running Waters via Finke River 4WD Route. Open continuously. Parking. No toilets. No fires. Camping permitted only at Ilpurla Aboriginal Community (toilets and showers available), 2 km to the east. ☎ Barry Abbott 08-8956 7902.

Inarlanga Pass ❽

This was an important watering point and ceremonial place for Western Arrernte people. Only men could travel through here on their way to Giles Springs, a men's ceremony place in the ranges. The cycads (*Macrozamia macdonnelli*) in this striking gorge are reminders of wetter times. They survive here and elsewhere in the ranges because the high cliffs provide shelter from the sun for most of the day. The species is classified as vulnerable because of its restricted occurrence and severely fragmented populations. Fire and illegal seed harvesting are the major threats to its survival.

4 km nature trail from Ochre Pits.

Kalarranga Lookout ❾

The lookout provides a splendid vantage point for viewing an extinct meander that may have been sculpted over thousands of years by Palm Creek, a tributary of the Finke River. The cliffs of Kalarranga create a rocky amphitheatre and can be seen via the 1.5 km walk to the lookout or on the more extended Mpaara Track, a 5 km circuit that explains in signs the Dreamtime stories of the area, including that of the nocturnal mpaara (tawny frogmouth).

Off Finke River, 1.5 km from information board. Open continuously. Parking. No toilets.

OCHRE

Ointment, paint, termite deterrent, magic potion – ochre has many ceremonial and practical uses in Aboriginal life. Depending on the iron content and its degree of oxidation, the clay ranges in colour from red through purple to yellow. Ochre is quarried mainly by men, who carried large lumps on their heads using hairstring cushions or formed the soft ochre into bricks for transportation. Ochre was a valuable commodity, traded for bush foods, hairstring, boomerangs, spears, featherdown and pituri (native tobacco). It is still used today for body and object decoration and to a lesser extent for trading.

Larapinta Trail ❿

When completed, the Larapinta Trail will run for some 250 km along the West MacDonnell Ranges all the way from Alice Springs to Mt Sonder. The track is currently divided into 12 sections, which can be tackled as individual day-walks, or as multi-day treks, by any reasonably fit walker. A 13th section has been proposed which would extend the track from Mt Sonder to Mt Razorback. Camp sites and basic facilities are provided along the more frequently used sections, although in remote areas, there are no facilities. At the time of writing, eight sections of the track had been opened: sections 1–3 from Alice Springs to Standley Chasm, and sections 8–12 from Serpentine Gorge to Mt Sonder. The remaining sections should be completed by 2001 or 2002 (see Larapinta Trail, p. 79).

Informative maps of each section of the Larapinta Trail are available from the Visitor Information Centre in Alice Springs.

Namatjira Monument ⓫

This stone cairn stands amid the exquisite scenery that inspired Albert Namatjira, commemorating this famous Aboriginal artist and the school of painting he inspired. If time allows this is a wonderful spot to stop and enjoy the vivid landscape made famous by Namatjira. (see Hermannsburg (Ntaria), p. 84).

Larapinta Dr, 1 km from Hermannsburg.

Ochre Pits ⓬

These rainbow-hued banks form the only ochre quarry open to the general public in the Alice Springs area. The Arrernte people still use the clay from these cliffs and therefore ask visitors not to touch the cliffs. The site is connected to Inarlanga Pass by a 4 km nature track, and there's a fine view of Mt Sonder (1380 m) about 1 km in from the pits.

Off Namatjira Drive, 110 km from Alice. Open during daylight hours. Lookout. Parking. Toilets. Picnic tables. BBQ.

LONG-LOST DUNNART

In 1993, prisoners working on the construction of the Larapinta Trail near Ormiston Gorge made a critical scientific discovery in a discarded bottle. Inside was a creature that was at first thought to be a mouse, but was later identified as a long-tailed dunnart, an animal that had been thought extinct for nearly a century. The central rock-rat, which is endemic to this area, was also rediscovered in 1996 after a 36-year absence and is now part of the Parks and Wildlife Commission's regular survey and monitoring program.

Ormiston Gorge ⓭

Campers who prefer to have a few home comforts such as hot showers should head for Ormiston Gorge, where they will find one of the more developed campsites in the West Macs. But the towering red walls that frame the waterhole on Ormiston Creek are tangible proof that humans can never upstage nature. The gorge dissects a ridge formed of Heavitree quartzite. Geological action has effectively thrown two layers of quartzite one atop the other here, which explains why the cliffs rise to almost 300 m – twice as high as many other gorges in the area. This is a popular swimming spot in the warmer months (though even then the water can be very cold) and there are a number of walks in the area, including a half-hour return track to Ghost Gum Lookout, perched 70 m above the waterhole. There's also a

Ormiston Gorge features some of the Red Centre's most dramatic scenery.

Palm Valley's red cabbage palms have survived here for thousands of years.

7 km loop of Ormiston Pound that takes walkers into the flat floor of the 10 km diameter pound, enclosed by the 300 m cliffs of the Heavitree and Chewings ranges.

Off Namatjira Dr, 135 km west of Alice. Open continuously. Parking. Toilets. Wheelchair access. Picnic tables. Gas BBQs. Fires not permitted. Camping, caravans permitted. Ranger station ☎ 08-8956 7799.

Palm Valley ⑭

The moist environment created by the water and shade of the region's gorges has allowed some plant species to survive in an otherwise inhospitable land. Palm Valley, in Finke Gorge National Park, shelters the world's only examples of the red cabbage palm. The 5 km Mpulungkinya (Palm Valley) walking track allows visitors to explore the stark contrast between the lush, palm-punctuated gorges and the arid plateau above. Palm Valley itself lies 6 km from the entrance to the park; picnic and camping grounds (1 km apart) are

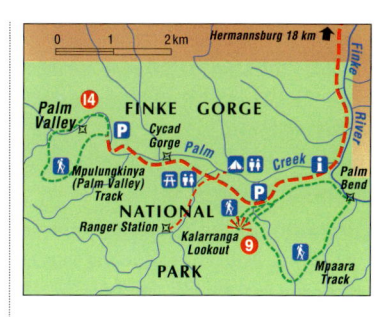

The waters of Redbank Gorge offer relief from the searing heat of summer.

located about 3 km in. The road is recommended for 4WDs only.

Off Larapinta Dr, 140 km south-west of the Alice, 20 km from Hermannsburg via Finke riverbed. Open continuously. Parking. Toilets. Picnic tables. BBQ. *Camping. Bring your own firewood. Ranger station* ☎ *08-8956 7401.*

Redbank Gorge ⓯

Ironically, the only time this narrow gorge is dry is following fierce floods, when tonnes of sand are dumped in it. It's a 25-minute walk along the creek to the waterhole at the entrance to the gorge. Visitors can swim there, though the water may be chilly even in midsummer. The carpark is the starting point for the 16 km return walk over rocky and steep terrain to the summit of Mt Sonder. Walkers who make it to the top are rewarded with awesome views of the West MacDonnells, the surrounding plains and to the west, the Territory's highest mountain, Mt Zeil. Mt Sonder was named in the early 1870s by explorer Ernest Giles' German patron Ferdinand von Mueller for a Hamburg botanist, Dr Otto Wilhelm Sonder. Some say this prominent peak resembles a reclining female figure. For the Western Arrernte, the mountain, which they call Rwetyepme, has great religious significance. As a result, they forbid camping and fires in the area. A 4WD-only road connects Redbank Gorge with Tnorala (Gosse Bluff) Conservation Reserve and Hermannsburg (Ntaria), and the Mereenie Loop Road to Watarrka National Park (see Reference Directory).

Off Namatjira Dr, 160 km west of the Alice. Open continuously.

West of Alice Springs

Parking. Toilets. Picnic tables. bbq. Camping. Bring your own firewood.

Running Waters ⓖ

Migratory and resident birds know a good hide when they find one and this waterhole, located on a cattle station just outside the Finke Gorge National Park, is no exception. Although the water is permanent, it's very shallow and surrounding cumbungi makes good cover for birds and their watchers. From here, the Finke River 4wd Route leaves the riverbed for Illamurta Springs and Watarrka National Park.

On Finke River, 28 km south of Boggy Hole. Open continuously. Parking. No toilets.

Serpentine Chalet Bush Camp ⓗ

When this camp was established by pioneering tourism operator Len Tuit in 1958–59, it took a full day's journey on a rough bush track to get there from the Alice. Today, the drive to the remnants of this rustic resort takes little more than an hour, but it's still 4WD territory beyond the ruins to the basic bush camping ground. From there, it's a 2 km walk to the dam that once serviced the chalet. The Larapinta Trail connects with the track at this point, and walkers may join it and head west for 2.3 km to cycad-packed Inarlanga Pass and a further 4 km to the Ochre Pits. Alternatively, they can head east for a more arduous 7 km walk to Serpentine Gorge.

Aboriginal legend tells of a wedge-tailed eagle that patrolled the area between Serpentine Gorge and the Ochre Pits during the Dreaming. The Arrernte people believe the eagle now lives in the range high above the gorge entrance, from where it guards against intruders.

Off Namatjira Dr, 108 km from the Alice. Open continuously. Parking. No toilets. Bush camping.

Serpentine Gorge ⓘ

As the name suggests, this gorge snakes its way through 2 km of the Heavitree Range. Its permanent waterholes provide a refuge for rare aquatic species such as the waterpenny, a small rock-clinging invertebrate with a segmented shell like a chiton, which appears to have survived from a much wetter era. The area also supports 16 rare and relict plants. Visitors can walk along the 1.3 km walking track to the first waterhole of the gorge. From there, a steep climb to a lookout provides a good view of the 300 m high ridges of the gorge and the surrounding ranges.

Off Namatjira Dr, 102 km from the Alice. Open continuously. Parking. Toilets. Picnic tables.

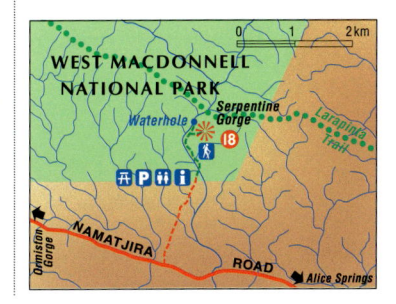

Simpsons Gap

Dawn and dusk are the best times to spot black-footed rock-wallabies on the scree slopes of the eastern bank of the gap gouged over the millennia by floods surging down Roe Creek. Swimming is not permitted in the small permanent waterhole but there are numerous walking opportunities, including the 8 km each way Woodland Trail to Bond Gap and the 23 km overnight walk along Section 1 of the Larapinta Trail (see p. 79 and p. 87) to the Alice Springs Telegraph Station. A sealed, 17 km bicycle path to the gap from Flynn's Grave (7 km from the Alice on Larapinta Drive) provides a great bushland ride for the whole family. Information signs along the path are great places to rest and discover more about the area (see Reference Directory for information on bike hire).

Off Larapinta Dr, 23 km from the Alice. Open daily, 8 a.m.–8 p.m. Parking. Toilets. Wheelchair access. Visitor Information Centre. Picnic tables. No camping permitted. Gas BBQs. ☎ *08-8955 0310.*

Standley Chasm

Expect crowds at midday, when the sun passing directly overhead ignites the 80 m high quartzite walls of this narrow slit in the West MacDonnells. The 1.5 km walk from the kiosk follows a rocky creekbed surrounded by cycads, ferns and river red gums. The opening is only 8 m wide at its narrowest and its shade provides one of four known habitats for the spring-flowering Centralian flannel flower (*Actinotus schwarzii*), which grows only in this area and the Petermann Ranges near Uluru. The site, named for Alice Springs' first school teacher, Ida Standley, is on Aboriginal land managed by the Angkerle Aboriginal Corporation. Seek permission from the kiosk before camping.

Off Larapinta Dr, 49 km west of Alice Springs. Open daily, 8 a.m.– 6 p.m. except Christmas Day. Parking. Toilets. Adults, $5.50; concession, $4. Kiosk. Picnic tables and BBQs. Limited camping. Kiosk ☎ *08-8956 7440.*

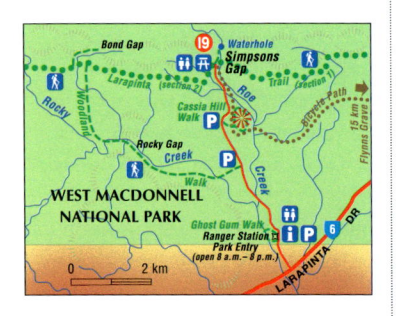

Simpsons Gap is a favourite watering hole for black-footed rock-wallabies.

Only at midday does sunlight penetrate the narrow recesses of Standley Chasm.

The 130-million-year-old meteor crater at Tnorala is an Aboriginal sacred site.

Tnorala (Gosse Bluff) Conservation Reserve ㉑

Aboriginal legend says that this basin was formed when a mother dancing across the sky put her baby down in a turna (wooden carrier) that toppled over and crashed to earth. Scientists say the crater, which is ringed by sandstone cliffs and 5 km in diameter, was formed 130 million years ago, when an extraterrestrial body (probably a comet) crashed to Earth with an impact equivalent to the force of 1 million Hiroshima-size nuclear bombs. Whichever story you subscribe to, the crater is an impressive sight. It would originally have been 2 km deep and 20 km across and is best viewed from the air or the trig station at Tyler's Pass Lookout, 22 km north on the high-clearance 2WD road to Redbank Gorge. The reserve is an important Aboriginal sacred site and the traditional owners don't allow camping or fires. Visitors require a permit, which also allows access to the Mereenie Loop Road.

183 km west of the Alice, 35 km off Larapinta Dr. Open sunrise to sunset. Parking. Toilets. Mereenie Tour Pass required, $2.20 from Glen Helen Resort (☎ 08-8956 7489); Kings Canyon Resort (☎ 08-8956 7442); Ntaria Supermarket, Hermannsburg (☎ 08-8956 7480) or the Central Land Council in Alice Springs (☎ 08-8951 6320). Picnic tables. No fires.

Twin ghost gums ㉒

Aboriginal artist Albert Namatjira brought these eucalypts, with their backdrop of the MacDonnell Ranges, into the living rooms of many Australian homes.

On Larapinta Dr, 19 km west of Alice Springs.

PINE GAP

Officially it's the Joint Defence Facility Pine Gap, but locals all refer to the US–Australian intelligence centre situated 30 km south-west of the Alice as "the space base". From the air, the 10 white radomes – environmental shelters for dish antennas – look like a cluster of giant golf balls in the desert. The facility, which is not open to the public, is a major employer in the Alice, with a staff of around 800. Almost half are American and are credited with introducing gridiron and baseball to the Red Centre.

Wallace Rockhole ㉓

Traditional Aboriginal paintings decorate buildings, rubbish bins and even the power poles in this community, which welcomes visitors and guides them to the rockhole of the settlement's name. The walls of this site feature petroglyphs (engravings) and hand stencils. Guided rock art tours explain their significance and locate other artefacts such as grinding stones. After the tour, groups can tuck into a meal of billy tea, damper and kangaroo tail roasted in traditional manner – bookings essential. The community's art room has local works for sale.

Off Larapinta Dr, 108 km from the Alice. Three or four tours daily. Parking. Toilets in camping ground. Adults, $7.70; children, $4; Picnic tables. BBQ. Store/fuel. Camping. *Two cabins, $75 per night each.* ☎ *08-8956 7993.*

Guided tours at Wallace Rockhole offer insights into traditional Aboriginal culture.

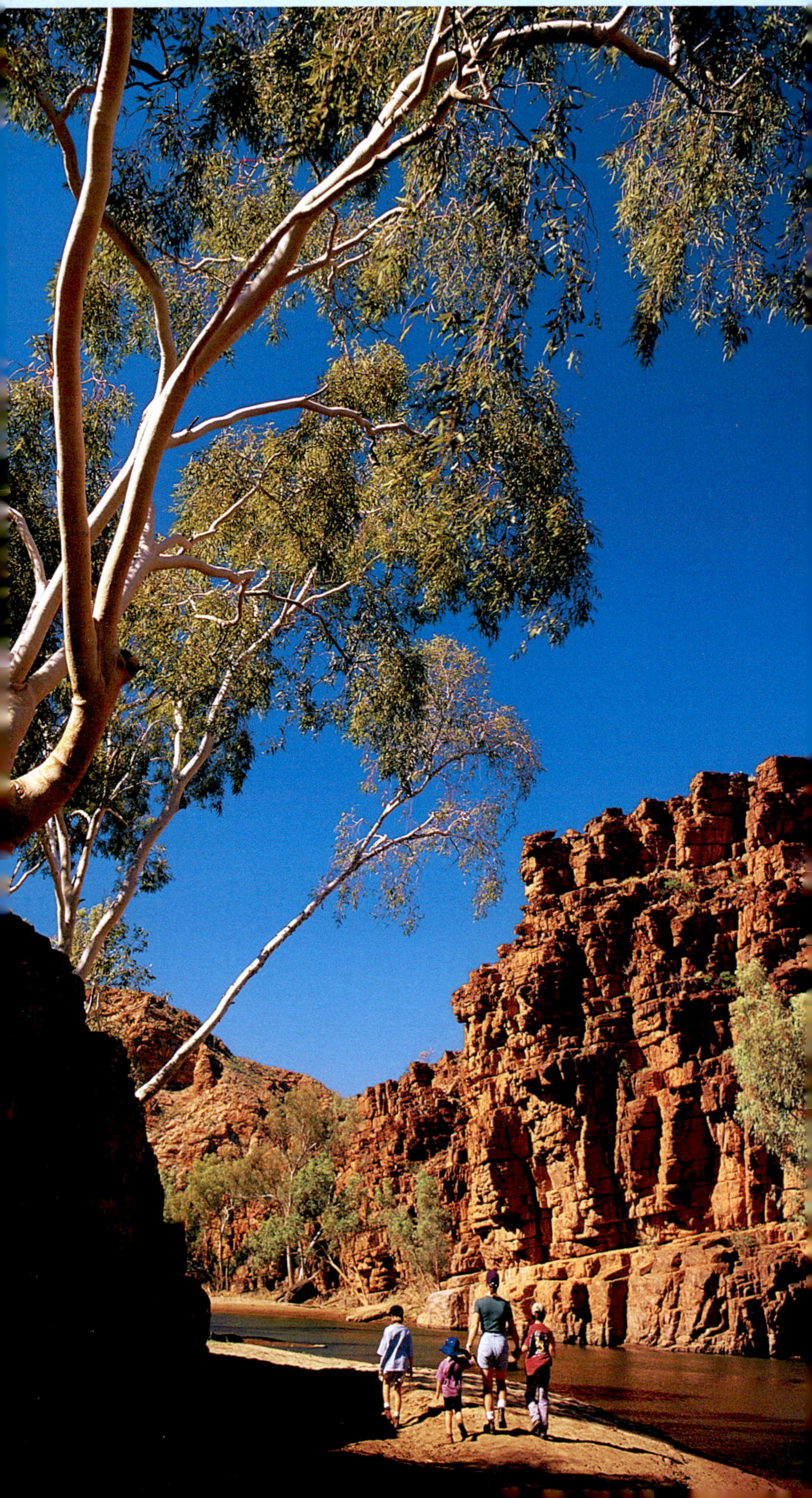

EAST OF ALICE SPRINGS

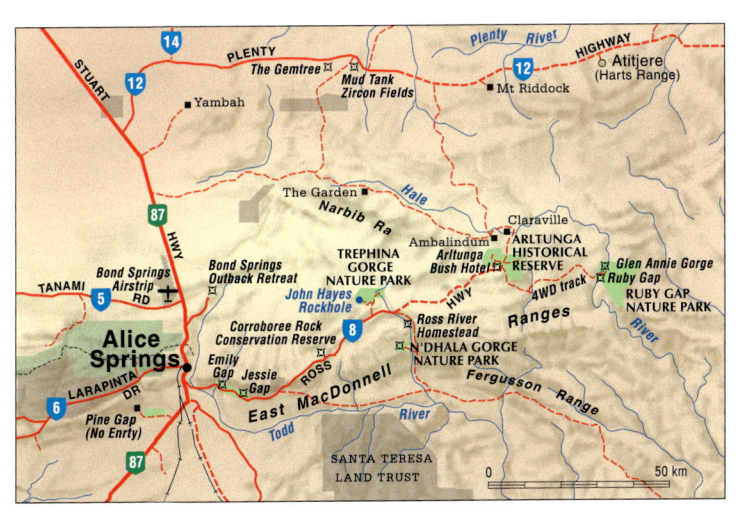

Ghost gums and soaring cliffs provide plenty of shade at Trephina Gorge.

East of Alice Springs

One long-time Red Centre park ranger says his favourite drive from Alice Springs is along the Ross Highway and into the dramatic gaps and gorges of the East MacDonnell Ranges. Although far less visited than the West MacDonnells, the ranges to the east are just as spectacular and equally interesting from both a cultural and historical point of view. The local Arrernte people believe that the Caterpillar ancestral beings came out of Emily Gap to form the entire MacDonnell Ranges, and there are numerous significant sacred sites located on a Dreaming track that runs through the East Macs. The history of European settlement is also commemorated here. Arltunga, the Red Centre's first town, has been preserved as a monument to the European miners who trudged with picks and wheelbarrows hundreds of kilometres into the unknown, seeking the gold that proved hard to find.

Arltunga Bush Hotel ❶

This "pub in the scrub" is an oasis for those exploring the East Macs and sells fossicking permits.

Open daily, 8 a.m.–10 p.m. BBQ. *Meals and ice available but no store, fuel or banking facilities. Fossicking permits. Basic accommodation; phone bookings essential. Camping, but no powered sites.* ☎ 08-8956 9797.

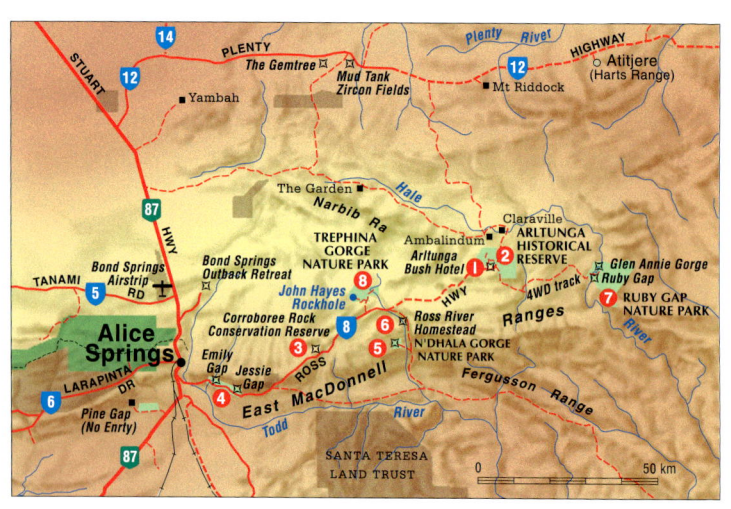

The brief but fascinating history of Arltunga is brought to life during guided tours.

ARLTUNGA HISTORICAL RESERVE FACT FILE

Elevation: 800
Population: 6
Location: 110 km east of Alice Springs, about one hour and 30 minutes drive. No public transport.
Police: (Harts Range) ☎ 08-8956 9772
Fire brigade: ☎ 08-8951 8279
Wildlife: contact ranger or ☎ 08-8951 8266
Visitor Centre: open daily 8 a.m.–5 p.m.
Information: ☎ 08-8951 8211
Toilets. Wheelchair access. BBQ. Picnic areas.

Arltunga Historical Reserve ❷

The Red Centre's first town rose out of the fields where gold was discovered in 1887 and at its peak, for a few months in 1903, its population numbered about 300. During World War II, an Aboriginal mission called Little Flower was moved here from Alice Springs. However, water shortages, sickness and high mortality resulted in its relocation to Santa Teresa in 1953. Today, Arltunga is a ghost town and a monument to the miners who played an important role in opening up the Red Centre. Visitors can explore restored buildings, stone ruins and scattered workings, and even crawl 6 m beneath the stony surface by

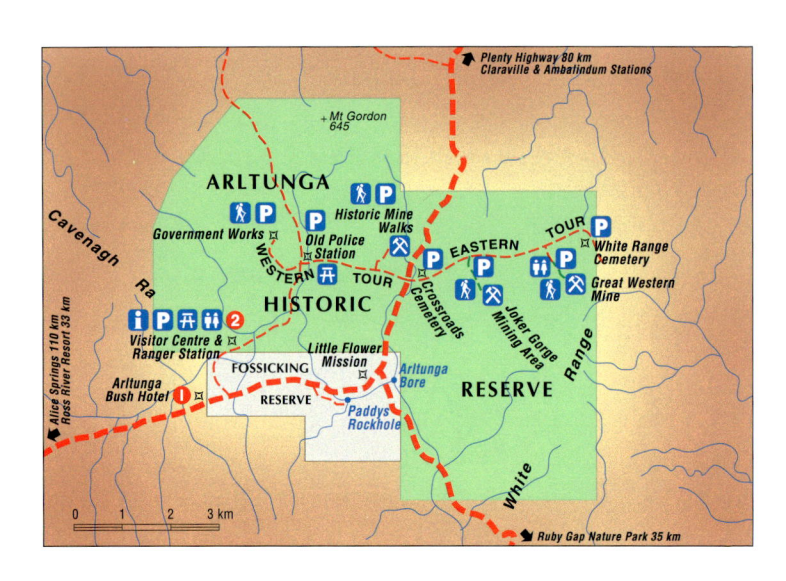

Most of the exhibits in Arltunga's visitor centre were retrieved from nearby mines.

way of the only underground mine (bring a torch). There are several self-guided walking tracks and rangers lead tours from May to September. Gold prospecting is not allowed in the historical reserve, but there is a fossicking reserve on its southern side.

Corroboree Rock Conservation Reserve ❸

This sacred Aboriginal site makes an interesting stop on the road east from Alice. You can read the signs about bush tucker before setting off on the 15-minute walk around the dolomite outcrop. Arrernte elders used the rock as a place to store secret sacred objects and would take younger men there to explain their significance. Camping is not permitted.

Walkers are asked to remain on the track at all times. Ross Hwy, 50 km east of the Alice. Parking. Toilets. Picnic tables. Information ☎ 08-8951 8211.

Emily and Jessie Gaps Nature Park ❹

Walking the 8 km ridge east from Emily to Jessie Gap – a great introduction to the East Macs – you're likely to be accompanied by soaring wedge-tailed eagles and may spot euros and rock-wallabies. Both mammals are of major significance to the Arrernte people. Emily Gap, a registered sacred site where the Caterpillar ancestors are said to have emerged to create the MacDonnell Ranges, has some fine rock paintings. Jessie Gap is more tranquil, but both are popular picnic spots and can be busy.

Ross Hwy, 10 km east of the Alice. Parking. Toilets. Picnic tables. Information ☎ 08-8951 8211.

N'Dhala Gorge Nature Park ❺

Signs help to interpret some of the Aboriginal petroglyphs, or rock engravings, for which this park is famous. About 6000 geometric symbols and animal tracks are etched into the broad rock surfaces. Many relate to the Caterpillar Dreaming that weaves its way through the East MacDonnell Ranges before turning south-east into the Simpson Desert. While walking along the rocky gorge, with its large ghost gums, listen for the many resident birds and look for native tomatoes and figs.

96 km east of the Alice (including 16 km of 4WD-only track south of

Corroboree Rock is sacred to the Arrernte.

Rock art at Emily Gap depicts the creation of the ranges by the Caterpillar ancestor.

At Glen Annie Gorge, the Hale River has exposed layers of red and white quartzite.

Ross River Homestead). *Parking. Toilets. Picnic tables.* BBQ. *Camping. Bring drinking water and firewood. Information* ☎ *08-8951 8211.*

Ross River Homestead ❻
Relax over a cool drink at sunset and chat with the locals at this friendly old homestead, which was one of the first in the Red Centre. Popular with coach groups as well as independent travellers, it is known for its billy tea and damper, as well as its horse and camel rides and demonstrations of boomerang-throwing and whip-cracking. There are also several marked walking tracks.

85 km east of the Alice. Open daily. Parking. Toilets. Wheelchair access. Restaurant/hotel (some supplies available). Cafe. Picnic tables. BBQ. *Fuel/email/stamps. Accommodation. Caravans (powered sites). Camping.* ☎ *1800 241 711.*

Ruby Gap Nature Park ❼
The walls of this park's southern gorge graphically illustrate the incredible forces of past mountain-building, when rocks were buckled, folded and squeezed like toothpaste. The discovery of what were thought to be rubies in 1886 led to a short-lived rush of eager prospectors until the "rubies" were shown to be less-valuable garnets. It's easy to understand the confusion: the river through Glen Annie Gorge seems to flow like red wine as the sun shimmers on the millions of garnet specks in its bed. The discovery of gold at Arltunga the next year drew many of the

You can sample all aspects of outback life during a stay at Ross River Homestead.

Serenity reigns at John Hayes Rockhole.

ruby prospectors. Upstream from Glen Annie a lonely headstone marks one of the Red Centre's first European graves, that of a miner named Fox who, presumably after failing to make his fortune, put an end to his life with his gun. The park has no facilities but is a bush camper's paradise and you can pitch your tent anywhere along the river. The Parks and Wildlife Commission warns not to drive onto the Hale River if the sand is soft and wet after rain. The river is also susceptible to flash flooding; if heavy rain falls, get out quickly.

150 km east of Alice Springs (Atnarpa Rd from Arltunga is high-clearance 4WD only). Parking. No toilets. BBQ. Camping. Information ☎ 08-8951 8211.

Trephina Gorge Nature Park ❽

Trephina Gorge's stirring scenery and great walking tracks make it one of the finest camping spots in the whole of the MacDonnell Ranges, and for many people this park is the star of the East Macs. The semi-permanent waterhole, in the sandy bed of a broad creek lined by river red gums, is rarely

---

FOSSICKING

"Eureka" fossickers often cry in the Red Centre, with its many areas of known gem and mineral deposits and more yet to be discovered. You will need a **Fossicker's Permit**, available from the Northern Territory Department of Mines and Energy (see **Activities, p. 38**) or its agents, where you can also pick up maps of designated fossicking areas. Agate, amethyst, apatite, epidote, beryl, **garnet**, **gold**, **jasper**, magnetite – these are just a few of the many riches waiting to be found. Fossickers are allowed to use hand tools such as picks, hammers, shovels, sieves and pans, can dig to a depth of 1 m and keep their **booty as long as** they're not involved in a commercial venture.

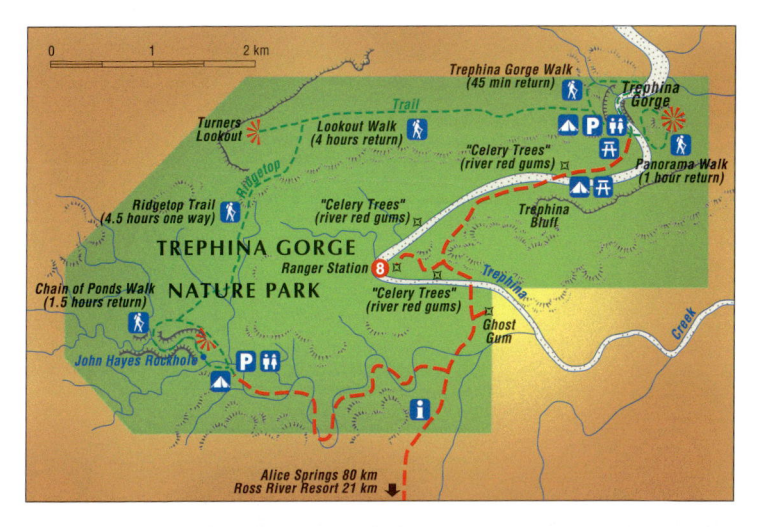

Trephina Gorge's semi-permanent waterhole is frequented by wildlife and campers.

full, but camping in the shade of the adjacent trees is a delight. Frequently seen wildlife includes the black-footed rock-wallabies that live among the quartzite rocks and many reptiles, dingoes and birds such as the striking Port Lincoln ringneck. The nearby John Hayes Rockhole, framed by striking red rocks, can be reached via a six hour 30 minute one-way walk or rough (4WD only) track.

85 km east of the Alice along the sealed Ross River Highway. Parking. Toilets. Picnic tables. BBQ. Camping. Bring your own firewood. Ranger campfire talks during peak season. Information ☎ 08-8951 8211.

106 THE RED CENTRE

SOUTH-WEST OF ALICE SPRINGS

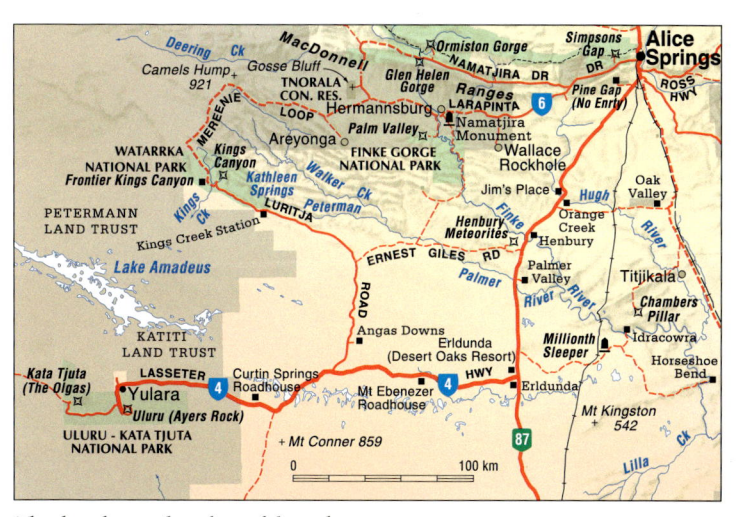

The sky takes on the colour of the rocks as the sun sinks behind a veil of cloud.

South-west of Alice Springs

Geologically speaking, the region south-west of the Alice has a wealth of riches. Three "rocks" – Uluru, Mt Conner and Kata Tjuta – loom over the landscape while to the north, Kings Canyon plunges dramatically into the earth. Yet when asked to nominate his favourite part of this region, one local ignored the obvious landmarks. "Kurkara (desert oaks)", he said, "seem to roll on forever." In fact, they're now mostly stationary. The scientists reckon that many have been in the same position for 30,000 years and it's only the loose sand on the crests that shifts in the wind. "And the night sky. Better than the fireworks on New Year's Eve. And we have it nearly every night."

The Finke River continues its journey across the Red Centre by diagonally bisecting this region. Once the highway from the south for missionaries and camel trains, today it's a beaten track for four-wheel-drivers on their way from Finke Gorge National Park to Watarrka National Park. The sealed Stuart and Lasseter highways provide the main access to Uluru and Kata Tjuta, while Lurijta Drive provides a sealed

The play of light and shade on the surface of Uluru creates an enchanting spectacle.

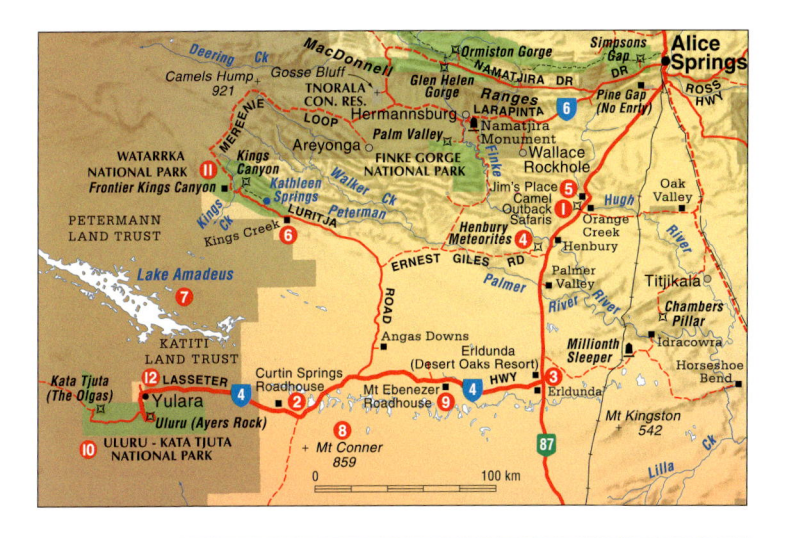

MEREENIE

Some 400,000 litres of oil are extracted daily from 30 wells at the Mereenie oil and gas fields, about 50 km north of Kings Canyon. The site, which also provides gas for electricity generation, is not open to the public, but travellers benefit from its existence because its access – the Mereenie Loop Road – provides an alternative route from Alice Springs to Kings Canyon. Unsealed, but usually accessible to conventional vehicles, the road crosses Aboriginal land and a permit is needed (see Essential Information, p. 48).

connection to Watarrka National Park. Although unsealed, the Mereenie Loop Road is usually negotiable for careful drivers of conventional 2WD vehicles, except after heavy rain. Not even locals take the unsealed Ernest Giles Road unless they have to, though the short section from the Stuart Highway to the Henbury Meteorites Conservation Reserve is usually accessible to all vehicles.

Ayers Rock
See Uluru–Kata Tjuta NP, p. 116.

Camel Outback Safaris
"Camel King" Noel Fullerton established the Territory's first camel farm in Alice Springs in 1972. He transferred the operation, now run by his daughter Michelle and her husband Crispin Gargan, to its present location 20 years ago. Rides range from five minutes to overnight and extended treks to Rainbow Valley. At the end of the year they also run a two-week safari to Palm Valley. Michelle and Crispin are both champion camel racers and

Curtin Springs station makes a fine base for exploring Uluru and Kata Tjuta.

HUBERT LEWIS (HAROLD BELL) LASSETER (1880–1931)

An extraordinary account of a fabulous gold find in the desert was just what Australians living through the Depression wanted to hear. Hubert Lasseter claimed to have discovered a 23 km long reef in the Petermann Ranges sometime between 1897 and 1911. In 1930, enough people believed him to fund a well-equipped expedition to the south-western corner of the Territory. The expedition turned back, but Lasseter stayed on and died of starvation in the Petermann Ranges in 1931. The story has inspired numerous follow-up expeditions, none of them successful. The Lasseter Highway from Erldunda to Uluru–Kata Tjuta National Park commemorates the prospector's optimism.

their mob includes Jessie, one of Australia's fastest camels.

Stuart's Well, on Stuart Hwy, 90 km south of Alice. Open daily except Christmas Day and Camel Cup (second Saturday in July), 7 a.m.–5 p.m. Parking. Toilets. Wheelchair access (disabled visitors are accompanied by an able-bodied rider). Cafe. ☎ 08-8956 0925.

Curtin Springs station ❷

Peter Severin had six visitors in 1957, the year he took over this 4166 sq. km cattle station named for Prime Minister John Curtin. In 1998, he and his son Ashley and grandson Steve welcomed 300,000 people to the roadhouse and accommodation on the Lasseter Highway, 80 km from Yulara. On tours of the station (with Ian Barker's Station Tours, operating from the roadhouse; see Reference Directory) visitors might see cattle, camels, dingoes, kangaroos and other wildlife as well as visit a salt lake, an early pioneer's dugout home and watch the sun set over Mt Conner.

On Lasseter Hwy, 365 km from the Alice. Service station and store open daily, 7 a.m.–11 p.m. Parking. Toilets. Wheelchair access. Licensed dining area. Picnic tables. BBQ. Store. Fuel. Demountable unit accommodation. Camping. ☎ 08-8956 2906.

Erldunda

Also known as the Desert Oaks Motel, this travellers' spot combines a motel, caravan park, tavern, store and service station for motorists journeying between the Alice and The Rock. There's a swimming pool, tennis court and fauna park, but otherwise not much to hold the visitor for more than an overnight stay.

Junction Stuart and Lasseter hwys, 200 km from the Alice. Service station open daily, 6.30 a.m.–10 p.m.; tavern open daily, 10 a.m.– 11 p.m. Parking. Toilets. Wheelchair access. Restaurant/cafe. Picnic tables. BBQ. Store. Fuel. Motel and budget accommodation. Camping. Caravan park. ☎ 08-8956 0984.

Henbury Meteorites Conservation Reserve

One of the Aboriginal names for this area translates literally as "sun walk fire-devil rock", which suggests that Aboriginal people may well have witnessed the meteorite shower that created this site around 5000 years ago. Fragments of the meteorites, composed of an alloy of nickel and iron, created 12 craters ranging from seven to 180 m in diameter. More than 500 kg of metal have been found on the site. One of the largest

Away from the main highways, services are sparse and roads can be rough going.

> ### JACK COTTERILL
>
> The corrugated-iron shed that Jack Cotterill built in 1958 must be living proof that "from little things big things grow". As a founding father of Red Centre tourism, Jack's shed was the first permanent accommodation at Uluru. After successful tours to Palm Valley and Uluru, Jack turned his attention in 1960 to Kings Canyon. He and his family cut a road to the canyon in 1960–61, built Wallara Ranch (now closed) to accommodate tourists and led tours of the region for 30 years. A cairn at the base of the Kings Canyon (the Rim) Walk commends Jack, who died in 1976, for his "foresight and effort".

Jim Cotterill maintains his family's tradition as outback tourism pioneers.

pieces, weighing 44 kg, can be viewed in the Central Australian Museum in Alice Springs.

Off Ernest Giles Rd, 145 km southwest of Alice, 13 km west of Stuart Hwy. Open continuously. Parking. Toilets. Picnic tables. BBQ. Camping.

Jim's Place ❺

The Cotterill family were among the early pioneers of tourism in the Territory. Jim Cotterill and his sons Craig and Phillip continue the tradition from their corrugated-iron-clad roadhouse on the highway south of the Alice. Located near the Orange Creek station homestead, this spot was renamed Stuart's Well because the explorer John McDouall Stuart drew water for his horses from an Aboriginal soak here. The walls of the roadhouse are hung with photographs chronicling the development of tourism in the Red Centre. A battered 1943 Dodge weapons carrier, used by Charles Chauvel during the making of the film *Jedda* and subsequently bought by the Cotterills for expeditions to Palm Valley and Kings Canyon, takes pride of place at the front of the service station.

Stuart's Well, on Stuart Hwy, 90 km south of the Alice. Open daily, 6 a.m.–10 p.m. Parking. Toilets. Wheelchair access. Licensed dining room. Picnic tables. BBQ. Store. Fuel. Cabins. Camping. Caravan park. ☎ 08-8956 0808.

Kings Canyon
See Wattarka NP, p. 125.

Kings Creek station ❻
"The adventure never ends," one Japanese visitor concluded after a stay with Ian and Lyn Conway on

South-west of Alice Springs 113

In its role as a camel station, Kings Creek even exports the animals to Saudi Arabia.

Helicopter rides from Kings Creek offer stunning views of the surrounding landscape.

their 1800 sq. km cattle and camel station. Helicopter flights, camel rides, station tours and the opportunity to mix with an outback family make this camping ground near Kings Canyon the sort of place where people come for a night and end up staying a week.

450 km from Alice Springs via Lasseter Hwy and Luritja Rd, 35 km from Kings Canyon. Open continuously, meals available 8 a.m.–7 p.m. Parking. Toilets. Wheelchair access. Dining room. Picnic tables. BBQ. Store. Fuel. Safari cabins. Camping. Caravan park. ☎ 08-8956 7474.

Lake Amadeus ❼

Lake Amadeus is a vast system of usually dry salt pans, the remains of the Amadeus Sea which covered most of Central Australia about 850 million years ago. Named by Ernest Giles after King Amadeus of Spain in acknowledgement of his patronage of science, this is the largest of Central Australia's salt lakes. Stretching more than 185 km, it is part of a much larger salt-lake chain that runs for over 500 km from Lake Hopkins in Western Australia almost to the Finke River. The best way to see it is from the air – weather permitting, Ayers Rock Helicopters (see Reference Directory) actually puts down on the northern shore.

35 km north of Yulara.

Mt Conner ❽

At first glimpse, many travellers mistake this table-topped hill for Uluru – at 344 m and 32 km around the base, it's a few metres shorter and 150 million years older than its more famous sibling. Mt Conner lies within Curtin Springs station, which is run by Peter Severin. Therre's a roadside lookout 21 km east of Curtin Springs Roadhouse, but the best way to get a close-up view of the mountain is with Uluru Experience from Yulara or Ian Barker's Station Tours from the roadhouse (see Reference Directory). It's a steep, but safe 2–3 hour climb to the summit, from which you can see Uluru and look across the borders to Western Australia and South Australia. Alternatively, take the easy option and land on its summit with Ayers Rock Helicopters (see Reference Directory). Local Aboriginal people know Mt Conner as Attila, but many call it Missus Mountain, a reference to the fact that the ashes of Peter's first wife Dawn were placed here.

Off Lasseter Hwy on Curtin Springs Station, 397 km from Alice. Accessible only with tour operators.

You can stock up with petrol, supplies and art at Mt Ebenezer Roadhouse.

Mt Ebenezer Roadhouse ❾

A gallery of Aboriginal paintings and craft makes this service station on the road to The Rock a worthwhile diversion. The artworks are all by artists from the nearby Imanpa community, which also owns the roadhouse.

On Lasseter Hwy, 256 km from Alice Springs. Open daily, 7 a.m.– 8 p.m. Parking. Toilets. Wheelchair access. Licensed dining room. Store. Fuel. Motel. Camping. Caravan park. ☎ *08-8956 2904.*

Usually a dry salt pan, Lake Amadeus contains surface water only after heavy rain.

Pleasingly symmetrical, Mt Conner rises steeply to its flat-topped summit.

EDDIE CONNELLAN (1912–1983)

Pioneer aviator Edward John Connellan first landed his aeroplane at the base of Uluru, on 7 August 1938. He started Connellan Airways (later Connair) as a mail and freight service to remote Territory communities in 1939, and began regular passenger services from Alice Springs to Ayers Rock in 1958. The airport at Uluru is named in his honour.

Uluru–Kata Tjuta National Park ❿

This is a World Heritage-listed reserve of 1325 sq. km protecting the iconic landforms of Uluru and Kata Tjuta as well as 24 native mammal species, 161 bird species and more than 560 plant species. In a landmark event in 1985, the Federal Government handed the park back to its traditional custodians, the Anangu people. It is now operated on a 99-year lease to Parks Australia and managed by a board of six Anangu and four non-Anangu members.

Make the Uluru–Kata Tjuta Cultural Centre, 1 km from Uluru on the main road from Yulara, your introduction to this area. The Mutitjulu Aboriginal Community, to the north-east of Uluru, is home to about 400 Anangu and is not open to the public. Camping and accommodation to suit all budgets is available at the purpose-built township of Yulara, 5 km from the park. Adult entry costs $15 for a three-day pass.

On Lasseter Hwy, 445 km southwest of the Alice. Opening times: December, January and

South-west of Alice Springs 117

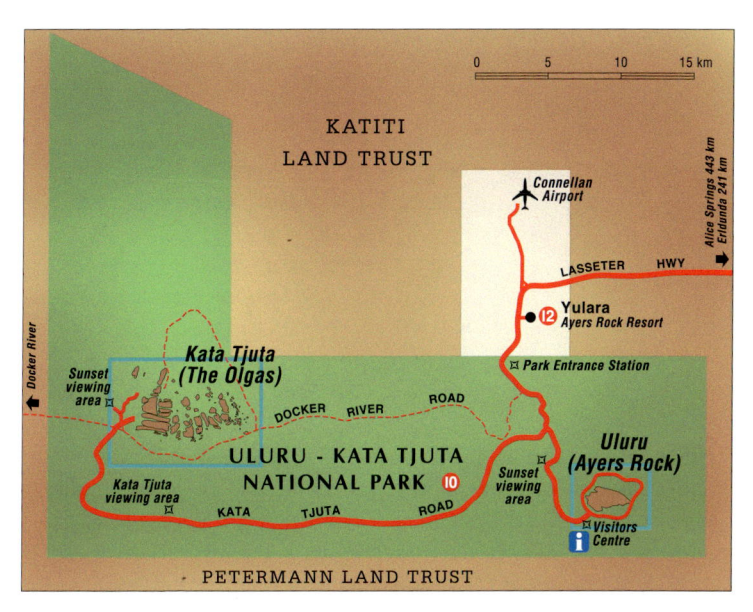

On the crest of a low dune, camel riders pause to admire the grandeur of Uluru.

NGANANA TATINTJA WIYA – WE DON'T CLIMB

The climb to the top of Uluru follows the traditional route taken by ancestral Mala men. The Anangu people would prefer that you respect the spiritual significance of the path and choose not to climb The Rock. They also feel a great sadness when people die or are injured on Uluru. A chain still lines the route for those who are determined to be minga (ants), but it is a steep path and you should not even consider the ascent if you suffer from a heart condition, respiratory problems or fear of heights. If you do choose to climb, be sure to follow the safety requirements and stay on the marked track. Carry plenty of water, wear a secure hat and sturdy, rubber-soled shoes.

February, 5 a.m.–9 p.m.
March, 5.30 a.m.–8.30 p.m.
April, 6 a.m.–8 p.m.
May, 6 a.m.–7.30 p.m.
June and July, 6.30 a.m.–7.30 p.m.
August, 6 a.m.–7.30 p.m.
September, 5.30 a.m.–7.30 p.m.
October, 5 a.m.–8 p.m.
November, 5 a.m.–8.30 p.m.

Uluru

In July 1873, explorer William Gosse became the first European to sight "one immense rock rising out of the plain". He named the monolith Ayers Rock, after Sir Henry Ayers, who was then Premier of South Australia, and in climbing the 348 m to the summit started a tourist procession that continues to the present day.

Anangu would prefer visitors didn't make the climb, which takes 2–3 hours return (and is closed after 8 a.m. on days when the temperature forecast is for above 36ºC, and when it's windy, raining or there is a possibility of a storm). As alternatives, they suggest a number of self-guided or accompanied walks that provide visitors with a better understanding of the land as well as the culture and beliefs of its Aboriginal owners.

The **Base Walk** stretches for 9.4 km around the edge of Uluru and takes 3–4 hours. Along the way, you'll come across ancient art sites as well as diverse plant and animal life. Uluru Experience offers an accompanied dawn walk with breakfast included, and Anangu Tours operates several Aboriginal-guided tours departing from the Cultural Centre (see Reference Directory).

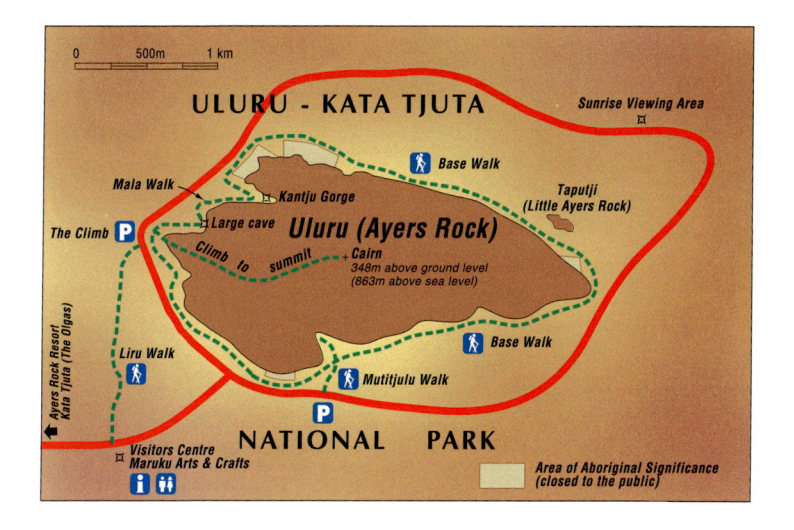

MALA DREAMING

The Mala (rufous hare-wallaby) people arrived from the west and north to hold an important ceremony. Some of the Mala men climbed to the top of Uluru to plant the Ngaltawata or ceremonial pole. People from the west arrived to ask the Mala to join another ceremony. The Mala refused as they had already started their own proceedings and the people from the west left, angry and insulted. As revenge, they sent Kurpany, an evil, dog-like creature, to attack the Mala. Despite a warning from Lunpa, the kingfisher woman, many Mala were killed and injured. The survivors fled to the south and south-east.

The **Liru Walk** (about 2 km, 2 hours return) follows a track from the Cultural Centre to Uluru; along the way, guides explain Tjukurpa (Dreaming) stories, and how to make kiti (bush glue), start a fire without matches and make wooden implements with stone tools. The **Kuniya Walk** combines an Aboriginal-led introduction to the Cultural Centre with a guided walk along the Mutitjulu Walk, visits to art sites and an explanation of bush tucker and desert survival, including a demonstration of the preparation of grass-seed flour.

The **Mutitjulu Walk** (a gentle 45-minute walk from the carpark, wheelchair access) goes to one of the few reliable waterholes at Uluru. There are daily ranger-accompanied tours of the **Mala Walk** (2 km one way, 1 hour return, wheelchair access) which leads from the Mala Walk carpark (also the base for the Uluru climb) to Kantju Gorge. Along the way,

Rainwater fills hollows in Olga Gorge.

rangers explain park management and Tjukurpa stories. From the waterhole, retrace your steps or continue on the Base Walk.

Harley Davidson bike tours, camel rides across the dunes, the Sounds of Silence gourmet dinner under the stars and helicopter or fixed-wing flights will all add new dimensions to The Rock experience. But don't forget to allow time to simply sit and soak up the sheer magnitude of the site, the splendour of its sunrise and sunset, the throat-catching beauty of its night skies, its almost tangible spirituality and its significance to those who are lucky enough to call this remarkable place home.

14 km from park entrance. Parking. Toilets. Wheelchair access at Mutitjulu and Mala walks.
☎ *08-8956 3138.*

Kata Tjuta

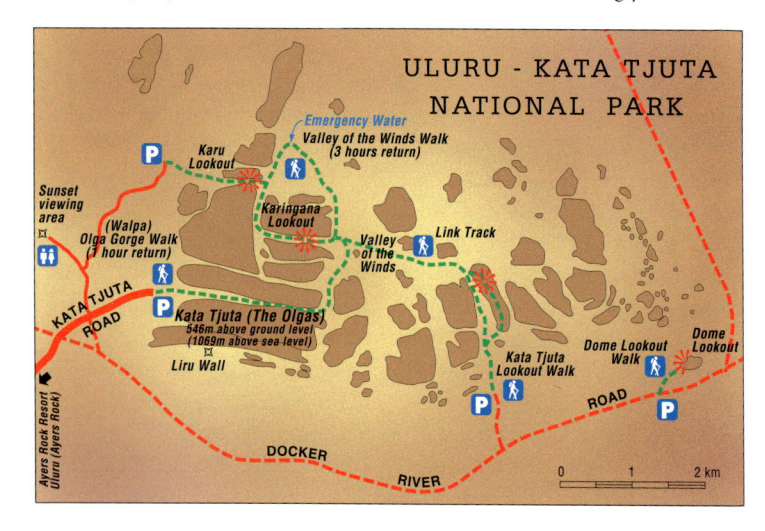

The name of this extraordinary outcrop translates as "many heads". Thirty-six domes make up the formations surrounding Mt Olga (1066 m), which was named from a distance after the Queen of Spain by explorer Ernest Giles in 1872. Although beaten by William Gosse to a close encounter with Kata Tjuta and Uluru, Giles returned the following year to describe Kata Tjuta as "solid rounded blocks of bare red-coloured stone, of a kind of conglomerate, being composed of untold masses of round stones of all kinds, mixed as plums in a pudding, and set in vast and rounded shapes upon the ground". The best way to appreciate these extraordinary formations and the gorges and valleys between them is on the **Valley of the Winds Walk**, a 7.4 km (about 3 hours) circuit that takes in two excellent vantage points – the Karu and Karingana lookouts. For visitor safety, this walk is closed after 11 a.m. on days when the temperature is forecast to reach 36°C or more. The Walpa, or Olga Gorge, Walk is a less taxing, 2.6 km (about 1 hour return) hike to the end of a gorge where spearwood vines flourish. Less visited but more varied than its more famous neighbour, Kata Tjuta also turns on a spectacular show at sunset.

47 km from park entrance. Parking. Toilets. Picnic tables.
☎ *08-8956 3138*

Uluru–Kata Tjuta Cultural Centre
The traditional owners of Uluru–Kata Tjuta provide insights into their culture at this centre through guided tours, arts and crafts, audio-visual displays and working demonstrations. The centre contains an information desk (☎ 08-8956 3138) for park notes and publications, information on tours, walks and ranger activities,

Kata Tjuta's jumble of domes inspired Giles to compare them to a plum pudding.

A visit to the Cultural Centre is the ideal way to start your tour of the park.

Ininti Souvenirs and Cafe (☎ 08-8956 2437), the exhibition and sales space of Maruku Arts and Crafts (☎ 08-8956 2558) and Aboriginal-operated Anangu Tours (☎ 08-8956 2123). Please respect the wishes of those Anangu who neither wish to be photographed nor to have any photography or video recording in the precinct.

1 km from Uluru on main road from the park entrance. Open daily, November–March, 7 a.m.–6 p.m.; April–October, 7 a.m.–5.30 p.m. Parking. Toilets. Wheelchair access. Cafe.

Watarrka National Park

The park covers an area of almost 72,000 ha at the western end of the George Gill Range. Watarrka is the Luritja name for the umbrella bush common to this rugged landscape and also for the area around Kings Canyon, the star attraction of the park. Watarrka features sheer sandstone walls soaring 150–200 m above the bed of Kings Creek, the beehive-like weathered domes of the Lost City, lush vegetation in the Garden of Eden, and more than 600 species of plants, of which 60 are rare or relict. The park is also home to about 60 reptile species

Red kangaroos graze among the cliffs and boulders of Watarrka National Park.

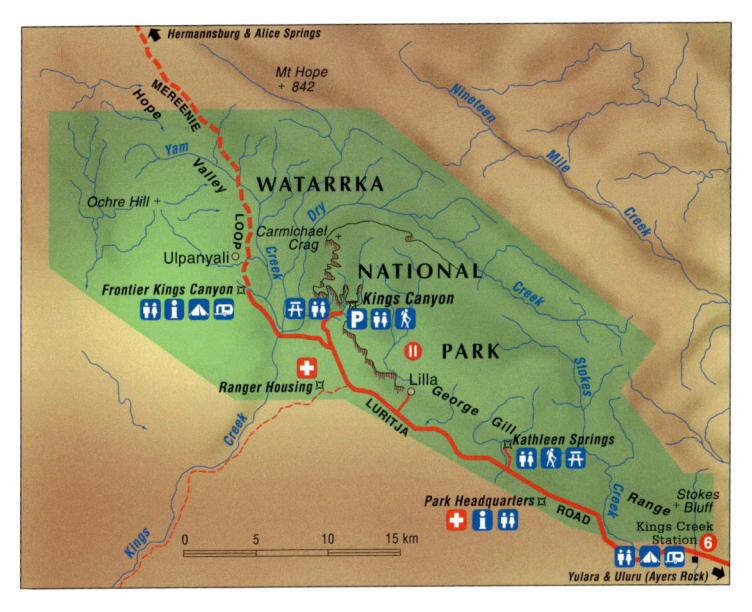

Viewed from the rim of Kings Canyon, the Lost City lives up to its name.

and populations of rock-wallabies, euros and red kangaroos. Walking, photography and birdwatching (more than 60 bird species, including the elusive, nocturnal tawny frogmouth, have been recorded here) are popular activities. Camping is not permitted within the park, though campers are welcome at nearby Kings Canyon Resort, as well as Kings Creek station, which lies just outside the park. Watarrka currently has no interpretive centre but visitors will encounter rangers out in the field and can contact them on ☎ 08-8956 7488.

480 km from the Alice via Stuart and Lasseter hwys and Luritja Rd. Open continuously.

The dramatic cliffs of Kings Canyon rise to 200 m from the valley floor.

Kings Canyon

With its sheer walls dropping 150–200 m to the valley below, Kings Canyon is one of the country's most spectacular and most photographed sights. An ad agency recently shipped in a youth choir to film a Qantas advertisement here and the producers of the film *Priscilla, Queen of the Desert* dressed actors in drag to shoot dramatic sequences on the clifftops. The canyon was formed by the erosive action of wind and water on Mereenie sandstone that was deposited about 360 million years ago. It is best explored via the 6 km **Kings Canyon Walk** which takes in the Garden of Eden, the domes of the Lost City, the ripple-stone remnants of an inland sea and the Southern Wall Lookout, from which you can see the whole gorge and a waterfall that runs when the creek floods.

Along the route, look for ghost gums (*Eucalyptus papuana*), which can be seen here in both their normal and dwarf forms. The **Kings Creek Walk**, about 700 m of which is wheelchair accessible, follows the boulder-strewn, waterhole-punctuated creekbed for about 1.5 km to a lookout. At the much less-visited **Kathleen Springs**, a 2.6 km disabled access track allows wheelchair-dependent travellers to go all the way to a spectacular rock pool – a registered sacred site – at the base of

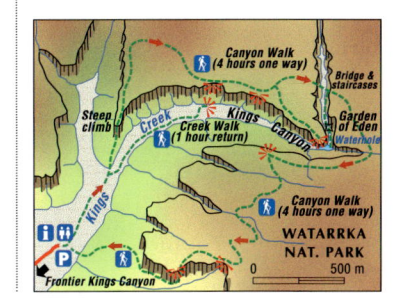

Descend into the canyon to explore the lush rockpools of the Garden of Eden.

Early morning walkers peer cautiously over the southern rim of Kings Canyon.

> When Ernest Giles stumbled across Kings Canyon in 1872, "Its springs, glens, gorges, ferns, zamias and flowers would charm the eyes and hearts of toil worn men who are condemned to live and die in crowded towns".

the range. The **Giles Track** is a 22 km overnight walk linking Kings Canyon with Kathleen Springs. Walkers must register with the Overnight Walkers Registration Scheme (see Essential Information, p. 48). Lilla Aboriginal Tours offers guided tours through an area rich in sacred caves and paintings at Lilla ("sweet-water rockhole"), 13 km from Kings Canyon Resort. The tours include talks on Aboriginal traditions and legends, and bush tucker and medicine, and conclude with boomerang- and spear-throwing lessons.

10 km from Kings Canyon Resort. Parking. Toilets. Limited wheelchair access. Picnic tables. BBQ. ☎ 08-8956 7488.

Kings Canyon Resort
Cradled in the lee of Carmichaels Crag, Kings Canyon Resort established new benchmarks for environmentally sensitive tourism when it opened in 1991. Accommodation options range from the hotel and budget lodge to a caravan park and camping ground. Ranger-conducted slide shows and star-gazing are popular night-time activities at the camping ground.

10 km from Kings Canyon. Open continuously. Parking. Toilets. Wheelchair access. Restaurant/cafe. Supermarket. Fuel. Camping. Caravan park. ☎ 08-8956 7442.

Yulara

The name of this purpose-built resort 12 km north of Uluru means "where dingoes howl". The entire township, which opened in 1984, was designed by celebrated Australian architect Philip Cox. No building is higher than the surrounding sand dunes and the colours are chosen to blend with the landscape. Water is pumped from underground bores and purified for human consumption and 70 per cent of the hot water supplied to the resort's three hotels, budget lodge, apartments, two camping grounds and staff quarters is solar-generated. Amenities include bars, restaurants, a bakery, supermarket, bank, post office, hair and beauty salon, and photo shop. A useful resort guide can be picked up from the Visitors Centre or from any of the hotel reception desks.

440 km from Alice Springs via Stuart and Lasseter hwys. Open continuously.

YULARA FACT FILE

Elevation: 500 m
Population: 1100
Location: 440 km from Alice Springs via Stuart and Lasseter hwys, about five hours drive from the Alice
Police: ☎ 08-8956 2166
Fire: ☎ 08-8956 2061
Medical centre: ☎ 08-8956 2286
Road service: ☎ 13 11 11
Wildlife rescue: ☎ (0418) 897 860
Tour and Information Centre:
Open daily, 8.30 a.m.–8.30 p.m.,
☎ 08-8956 2240
Visitor Centre: Open daily, 8.30 a.m.–7.30 p.m., ☎ 08-8957 7377
Public transport: Free shuttle bus does a 20-minute circuit around Yulara, stopping at hotels, the shopping centre and camel farm
Transfers to Uluru and Kata Tjuta:
Uluru Express ☎ 08-8956 2152 and AAT Kings ☎ 08-8956 2171
Free shuttle bus to Connellan Airport: AAT Kings ☎ 08-8956 2171

A steady stream of tour buses plies the highway between Yulara and the main sights.

128 THE RED CENTRE

South-east of Alice Springs

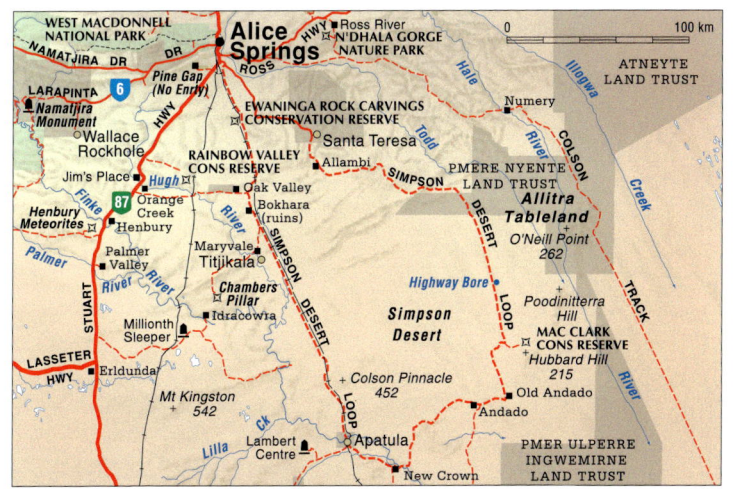

Exploring the Simpson Desert requires a 4WD and thorough preparation.

South-east of Alice Springs

Remoteness permeates everything in this region, where the rugged landforms and surprising vegetation of the Red Centre gradually give way to desert sandplains and dunes. The Simpson Desert Loop, which takes in many of the points of interest and dips into South Australia, is regarded by many as one of the country's great 4WD trips. Here, perhaps more than anywhere else in Central Australia, you will feel the wild, untamed spirit of frontier country which even many birds and native animals seem to eschew. After rain, hardy travellers are rewarded with one of the greatest shows in the Red Centre – a magic carpet of wildflowers.

Apatula (Finke)

Finke, a railway town built on the Finke River in the late 1920s, was an important fuel and water stop for the old Ghan, and now, as Apatula, is an Aboriginal community of more than 200 people. No permits are required to visit this town, which was the first stop in the Territory for the old Ghan, but it is a dry community and alcohol is not permitted. It's an interesting place to stretch your legs before or after the rigours of driving more than 100 km through 5–8 m sand ridges on the loop north. The grave of James McFarlane, who accidentally shot himself in 1881 while visiting Charlotte Waters, is 21 km to the south.

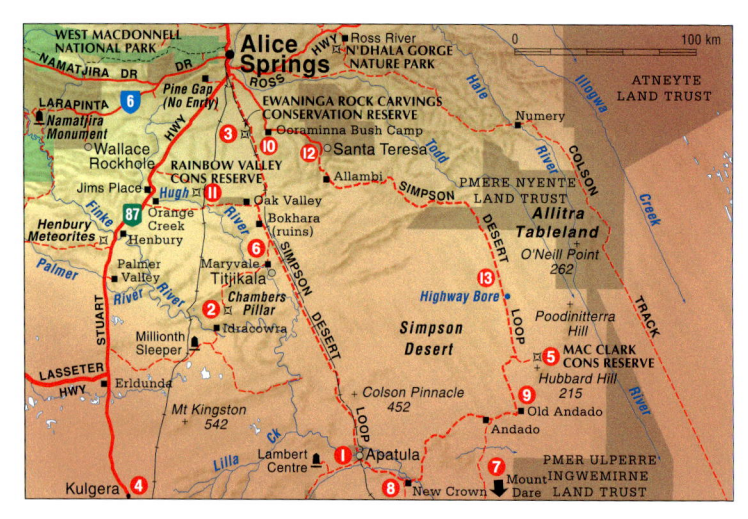

Following rain, wildflowers burst into bloom across the normally barren plains.

235 km south of the Alice on Simpson Desert Loop or 422 km south of the Alice via Stuart Hwy and Kulgera. Store (hot food). Fuel. No camping in town. Bush camping on Aboriginal land nearby (must be left as found). ☎ 08-8956 0966.

Chambers Pillar Historical Reserve ❷

The astonishing colours of the Red Centre seem to radiate from this vertical 50 m finger of sandstone, especially at sunrise and sunset, which makes it an impressive campsite. Understandably for such a prominent navigational landmark, the pillar is important in Aboriginal and European history. Aboriginals call it Itirkawara, after a gecko ancestor who took a bride of the wrong relationship or "skin group" and became the pillar. The girl, turning her face away from him in shame, became nearby Castle Rock. Explorer John McDouall Stuart named Chambers Pillar after one of his backers, and other Europeans, including Ernest Giles and Overland Telegraph Line pioneers John Ross and Alfred Giles, are known to have passed it. Before the advent of rail transport in the 1920s, those on the long journey from Adelaide to Alice Springs knew, when they got to the pillar, that they had almost reached their destination.

160 km south of the Alice, 4WD only from Maryvale station. Parking. Toilets. Picnic tables. BBQ. Camping. ☎ 08-8951 8211.

Ewaninga Rock Carvings Conservation Reserve ❸

The sandstone outcrops around a small claypan made this a favourite stopping place for Central

A rich array of carved motifs decorates the rocks of Ewaninga Conservation Reserve.

THE GHAN

Heavy timber sleepers and a few warped sections of track are all that remain of the old Ghan railway line, which was responsible for opening up much of the Red Centre. Nowadays, you can even drive on the old rail bed, if you can bear the corrugations. The first train, named after the "Afghan" cameleers it replaced, arrived in Alice Springs on the narrow-gauge line from the railhead at Oodnadatta in 1929. The heavily subsidised fortnightly service was often under threat of closure. Today's standard-gauge line, west of the original, opened in 1980, creating a string of ghost towns and sidings along the former line. Travelling by train from southern cities to Central Australia on The Ghan is considered one of the great rail journeys of the world.

Australia's first inhabitants. They covered the stone with carvings now believed to be among the oldest in the Centre. Their meaning is sacred and considered too dangerous to reveal, even to non-initiated Aboriginals. Their age, if known, also remains a secret; European estimates vary from 1000 to 20,000 years. Signs along the self-guided walk explain the site's significance, a key rain-making area for the Eastern Arrernte.

35 km south of the Alice. Parking. Toilets. Picnic facilities. ☎ 08-8951 8211.

Kulgera

The Kulgera Hotel Motel and police station are the only

residences in this first stop on the Northern Territory side of the border with South Australia.

On Stuart Hwy, 274 km south of the Alice. Open daily, 6 a.m.–midnight. Toilets. Restaurant/cafe. Picnic tables. BBQ. Basic store/EFT-POS. Fuel. Most major fuel cards. Motel rooms. Caravans (powered sites). Camping. ☎ 08-8956 0973.

Mac Clark Conservation Reserve ❺

Aboriginals made fighting clubs called waddies from the dense timber of *Acacia peuce*, or waddy-wood, which grows in abundance in this reseve. This is one of Australia's most striking trees and its wood is so hard that it resists nails. The species has a reputation as a tenacious survivor and grows in only two other places – both on the Queensland side of the Simpson Desert. About 1000 specimens grow to about 17 m here, in one of the hottest, driest parts of the country (average rainfall 150 mm). Named after the late Mac Clark of Andado station, who had a profound interest in these wattles, the reserve also contains some extensive archaeological sites. Stone tools and small hearths have been found near temporary waterholes in the main stand of trees.

40 km north-east of Old Andado, on the edge of the Simpson Desert. No facilities.

Maryvale station ❻

Many travellers to Chambers Pillar refuel at this friendly working cattle station, which has a store used largely by people from the nearby Aboriginal community.

107 km south of the Alice. Toilets. Store. Fuel. ☎ 08-8956 0989.

Mount Dare ❼

Located about 10 km beyond the South Australia border, this homestead of a former cattle station, now within Witjira National Park (see Further Afield), is an oasis for travellers on the Simpson Desert Loop and those preparing to set off on longer trips into the desert.

About 110 km south of either Apatula or Old Andado (depending on which way you are travelling the

The hard cap atop Chambers Pillar helped it resist years of weathering.

loop). Open year-round. Parking. Toilets. Light meals at bar. Picnic tables. BBQ. Store. Fuel. Accommodation for 14 in former homestead. Camping. ☎ *08-8670 7835.*

New Crown station ❽

Just over 30 km south of the homestead on this privately owned cattle station, on the road to Mount Dare, are the ruins of the Charlotte Waters Telegraph station, the departure point for several expeditions westward.

32 km south-east of Apatula. Fuel available in emergencies. ☎ *08-8956 0969.*

Old Andado ❾

This original five-room corrugated-iron and timber homestead was built in 1922 by the pioneers who had taken up the land in 1911. Molly Clark, who moved to the

---

SAND DUNES

From an aircraft, the dunes of the largest sand-dune desert in the world seem like tresses of hair streaming in the wind. The Simpson's dunes do, in fact, show the direction of prevailing winds in the Red Centre as far back as 25,000 years ago, when inland lake levels dropped and the world entered another ice age. Sand blown onto the downwind shores of lakes was later picked up by gales and flung even further downwind, forming the long, parallel dunes that run nor'-nor'-west from South Australia into the Northern Territory. Some are 200 km long and in the east can rise to 15 m.

Guests enjoy the sunset from their rustic accommodation at Ooraminna Bush Camp.

MOLLY'S BASH

On Mother's Day each year since 1993, Molly Clark of Old Andado, on the edge of the Simpson Desert, has opened her resort home for a fundraiser in aid of the National Pioneer Women's Hall of Fame. "Everyone's trying to get out of the rat-race," she says of the annual 400-plus crowd. "It makes me laugh." There's a treasure hunt, bush concert and a spit-roast banquet.

property with her husband Mac in 1955, saved it from being razed when Andado station was sold, and has restored it in 1920s–1930s style, though "with a few comforts – like power", Molly confides. Most people, however, including many overseas visitors, come to see legendary Molly as much as her resort, and she is happy to dole out some outback hospitality and chinwag over a meal.

315 km south-east of the Alice. Open March–November. Toilets. Dormitory accommodation for 10 (bookings essential). Meals (bookings essential). Caravans (powered sites). Camping. ☎ 08-8956 0812.

Ooraminna Bush Camp

Red sandhills and rocky outcrops provide a dramatic backdrop for visits to this tourist facility on a working cattle station. The bush camp offers a "Pub in the Scrub" day tour, which includes campfire food and entertainment, and an overnight package including dinner, swag and breakfast. Guests can also ride horses and take a trip to nearby Chambers Pillar. All tours include transport from Alice Springs; independent travel is discouraged because of the rough and fragile nature of the terrain.

30 km south of the Alice. Bookings essential. ☎ 08-8953 0170.

LAMBERT CENTRE

John McDouall Stuart's quick field calculations placed Central Mount Stuart, 212 km north of present-day Alice Springs, within 4 km of his estimated geographical centre of Australia. When the Royal Geographical Society of Queensland asked the Queensland Department of Geographical Information to calculate Australia's theoretical centre of gravity, the pivotal point where the continent would balance, they came up with Lambert Centre, named after a former head of the Division of National Mapping. Where is it? At latitude 25°36'36.4"S and longitude 134°21'17.3"E, about 22 km west of Apatula (Finke), 220 km south of Alice Springs, and 425 km south of Central Mount Stuart.

Rainbow Valley Conservation Reserve

As the setting sun moves over the bluffs and cliffs of Rainbow Valley in a light-show to rival that of Uluru, it tells a story millions of years in the making. The rainbow-like bands are the result of long weathering of the original Hermannsburg Sandstone. Red iron oxides leached from the deeper layers were deposited in the upper layers by wet season floods. When the water evaporated, the oxides formed the resistant, red layer near the top of the cliffs, which pales to yellow further down and white at the bottom, where the iron has been removed. The visual spectacle is most dramatic after rain, which intensifies the colours. The reserve, part of the James Ranges, is also rich in Aboriginal associations, featuring rock engravings

At sunset, the rocks of Rainbow Valley glow like the hot coals of a campfire.

and paintings, as well as grooves in the rocks where stone axes were ground. It's surrounded by spinifex sandplains and claypans. This is hot country, with little shade, so equip yourself accordingly.

100 km south of Alice Springs (78 km on Stuart Hwy, followed by 22 km on gravel road; a 4WD is recommended). Parking. Toilets. Picnic tables. BBQ. Camping. ☎ 08-8951 8211.

Varying amounts of iron oxide create the coloured bands in Rainbow Valley's cliffs.

Travellers should check road conditions locally before setting off into remote areas.

Santa Teresa

No permits are required to stock up at the shop or top up with fuel at this Aboriginal community, where the Roman Catholic mission that moved here from Arltunga in 1953 still operates. If you wish to linger, a permit from the Central Land Council is required and an appointment is necessary to view the works in the art gallery.

80 km south-east of the Alice. Store. Fuel. ☎ 08-8956 0805.

The Simpson Desert Loop

This popular, 760 km-return 4WD adventure takes travellers from Alice Springs through a timeless landscape and into the parallel sand ridges of the Simpson Desert. It can be travelled in either direction. The stretch from Alice to Apatula, where the loop crosses the Finke, follows the route of the old Ghan and is 4WD only. Most travellers divert to Chambers Pillar, which adds about 120 km to the circuit. Others, especially those coming from the south, turn off the Stuart Highway at Kulgera for Apatula and use either the eastern or western sections of the loop as an alternative route to the Alice, sometimes returning the other way. The western arc may be negotiated by 2WD with care.

LESSER BILBY

The small, long-eared burrowing bandicoot known as the lesser bilby is presumed extinct, despite a skull being found in an eagle's nest near the Simpson Desert Loop in 1967. No further evidence has been found of this agile creature, which had the long snout and powerful back legs of its better-known cousin.

Formerly a Roman Catholic mission, Santa Teresa is now an Aboriginal community.

140 THE RED CENTRE

NORTH OF ALICE SPRINGS

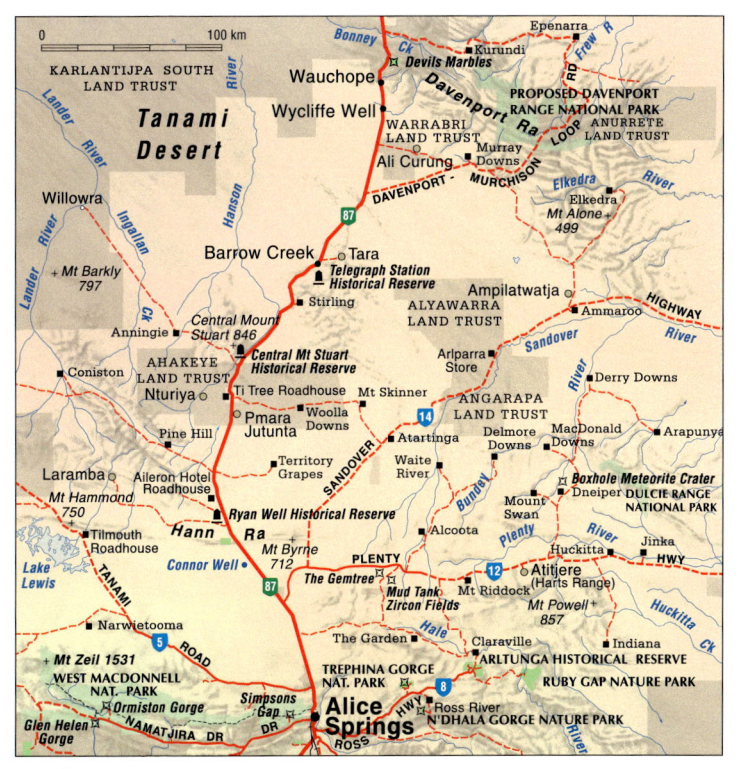

The tiny settlement of Barrow Creek began as a telegraph repeater station.

NORTH OF ALICE SPRINGS

It's wrong to think of the long haul along what is known as The Track – the Stuart Highway between Alice Springs and Darwin – as a penance for good times had in the Red Centre. In fact, you're clocking up the kilometres on a route through history – geological, Aboriginal and European – featuring rewarding stops and detours all along the way.

As the Overland Telegraph headed north, its wells became a survival chain for northward pastoral expansion and its repeater stations bases for permanent settlement. There were rushes for gold and other minerals, massacres and bloody retaliations; convoys of troops arrived during World War II and hordes of travellers have followed ever since.

North of Alice Springs

The weathered boulders of the Devils Marbles date back 1700 million years.

Heading north, the flat, tree-dotted plains of the Red Centre's mulga woodlands gradually dissolve into the lush, tropical greenery that characterises the Top End. All along the route, there's a good chance of spotting wild camels, kangaroos, inquisitive dingoes and harried-looking emus. Look up and you might see a wedge-tailed eagle soaring in thermals high overhead. The rocks and outcrops you will pass are among the oldest in Central Australia, created as long as two billion years ago. True believers in extraterrestrial life and those willing to suspend disbelief should visit the murals of UFOs at Wycliffe Well, considered one of the world's main spotting sites.

Aileron Hotel Roadhouse ❶

There is an up-market family restaurant, a popular swimming pool, a children's playground and kangaroos and emus at this regular stop on the Stuart Highway.

On Stuart Hwy, 133 km north of the Alice. Open daily, 6 a.m.–10 p.m. Parking. Toilets. Restaurant/cafe/bar. Picnic tables. BBQ. *Store.* EFTPOS. *Fuel. Motel/backpackers accommodation. Caravans (powered sites). Camping.* ☎ *08-8956 9703.*

Barrow Creek ❷

As he lay dying following an Aboriginal attack on the telegraph station here in 1874, postmaster James Stapleton exchanged morse code messages with his wife in Adelaide. Scores of Aboriginals

Expansive mesas characterise the landscape around Barrow Creek.

died in reprisals. The telegraph station at Barrow Creek, the first to be built north of Alice Springs, was completed two years before the fatal attack. The Overland Telegraph Line's overseer Charles Todd expected the station, located at the base of the picturesque Forster Range, to become "the nucleus of a thriving settlement". More than 125 years later, Barrow Creek's population has reached the grand tally of six. The telegraph station, which later became a ration depot, police station and military staging camp, has been carefully restored (ask for keys at the nearby hotel, built by Territory identity Joe Kilgariff in 1932). The adjacent blacksmith's shop was used as a jail, and two trees are registered Aboriginal sacred sites.

On Stuart Hwy 284 km north of the Alice. Barrow Creek Hotel open daily, 7 a.m.–11 p.m. Parking. Toilets. Wheelchair access. Cafe/restaurant. Picnic tables. BBQ. *Fuel. Caravans. Camping (pets permitted, including snakes and camels).* ☎ *08-8956 9753.*

Bond Springs Airstrip ❸

This alternative airstrip for Alice Springs is also used by gliders and ultra-lights. About 10 km further on, travellers heading north pass the Tropic of Capricorn marker.

20 km north of the Alice.

Bond Springs Outback Retreat ❹

Guests here have the chance to sample life on a working outback cattle station amid some of the oldest and best-preserved rural buildings in the Red Centre. The first family to live in the one-roomed homestead, built of poles with a rough stone floor and corrugated-iron roof in the 1870s, took a year to get here from Adelaide. Today's visitors to this award-winning retreat come from all over the world and stay in three elegant homestead guest rooms or in cottages in the grounds, and enjoy walks, birdwatching, swimming, tennis and touring.

18 km north of Alice Springs. Open all year. Bookings essential. ☎ *08-8952 9888.*

Boxhole Meteorite Crater ❺

The same exploding meteorite that blasted the landscape at Henbury Meteorites Conservation Reserve (see p. 111) may also have created this single, large, circular crater that measures approximately 200 m in diameter. The difference between this formation and those at Henbury is that here

---

WORLD SOLAR CHALLENGE

When adventurer Hans Tholstrup and motor-racing identity Larry Perkins crossed Australia from west to east in a fragile solar-powered vehicle in 1983, few would have predicted that the journey would evolve into one of the world's most prestigious solar-car races. Four years later, 23 vehicles from seven countries set off from Darwin for Adelaide in the first World Solar Car Challenge, in which the General Motors Sunraycer achieved an average speed of almost 67 km/h. A new record was set by Honda in 1996, its vehicle achieving an average speed of nearly 90 km/h. In October 1999, 42 vehicles from 11 nations competed in the 3000 km event.

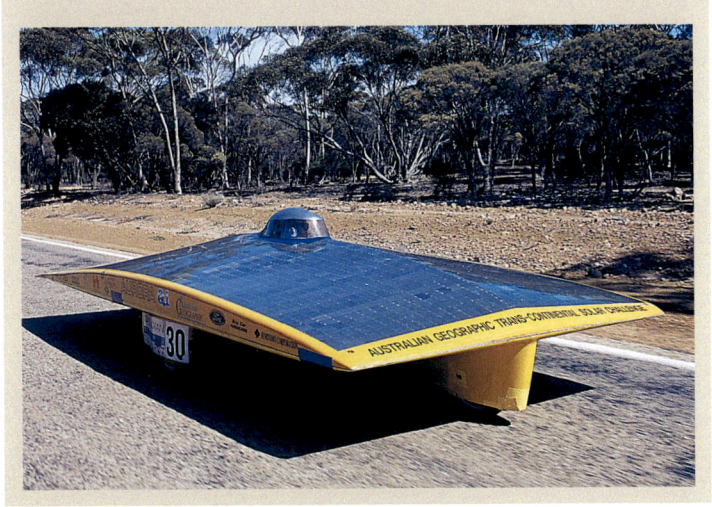

you can drive right up to the crater and sit on its rim. Iron fragments have been found scattered all over the impact site, which lies about 100 m from Dneiper homestead. Permission from the station owners is required to camp at this off-beat, privately owned site.

On Dneiper station, 270 km north-east of the Alice (about 37 km north of Plenty Hwy). No facilities. ☎ 08-8956 9849.

Central Mount Stuart Historical Reserve ❻

This tiny reserve and cairn beside the Stuart Highway commemorates John McDouall Stuart's climbing of nearby Central Mount Stuart, a somewhat uninspiring peak, which Stuart, however, calculated to be some 4 km from the geographical centre of Australia, in April 1860. "I wish it had been in the centre," he said of the spinifex-covered 849 m dome (see also Lambert Centre, p. 136).

On Stuart Hwy, 212 km north of the Alice. Parking. No toilets. ☎ 08-8951 8211.

Davenport Range National Park (Proposed) ❼

About 850 million years ago, when the Amadeus Sea swept across the Red Centre, probably only the site of Tennant Creek township and the Davenport Range emerged as rocky islands above its warm water. This 1120 sq. km park, renowned for its permanent waterholes, protects an important environmental zone between the tropical Top End and the Red Centre and marks the boundary between the traditional lands of the Warumungu, Alyawarr, Kaytetye and Wakaya peoples.

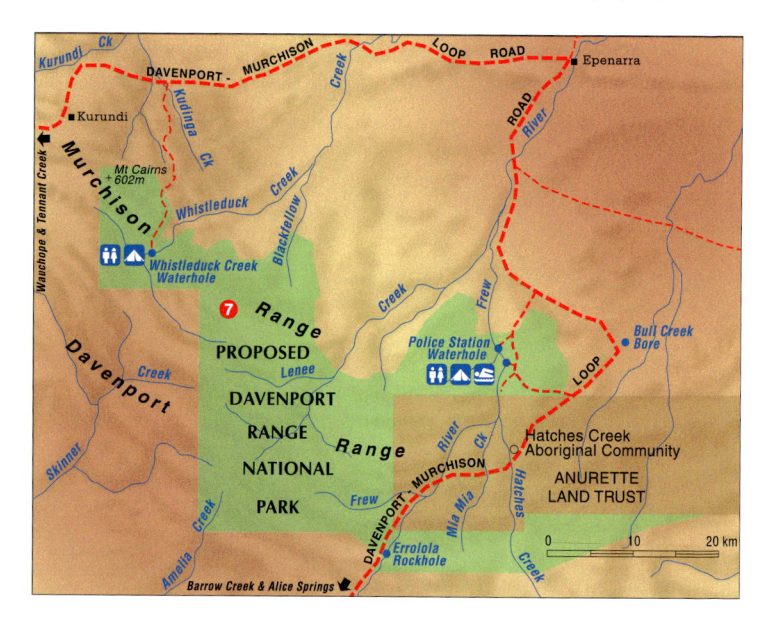

The Old Police Station Waterhole is the largest of Davenport's permanent pools.

It is one of the least-visited parks in the Northern Territory and its many waterholes make it a bushwalker's delight. They harbour at least seven species of fish, even though they are isolated from any other river system. Among the rare, endangered and significant plant species found in the park is the Davenport morning glory, which grows only here. Entering the park from Bonney Creek, visitors pass Kurundi station, which has a small store and campsite, and sells fuel. Its owners have devised a 130 km self-drive tour of the park, for which they sell maps and a cassette. Inside the park, there are campsites at the Old Police Station Waterhole, Whistleduck Creek and on the shores of the Frew River.

About 500 km north of the Alice via Stuart Hwy and Taylors Creek entrance (4WD only) or about 583 km north of the Alice via Stuart Hwy and Bonney Creek entrance (high road-clearance essential). Parking. Toilets. Picnic tables. BBQ. Camping. ☎ 08-8962 3388.

Devils Marbles Conservation Reserve ❽

Photographs capturing one or two of these dramatic formations, which have the appearance of modernist sculptures, never fully prepare people for the grandeur of this spectacular Red Centre landmark. The site consists of thousands of such boulders, measuring up to 6 m in diameter and stained orange-red by iron and other minerals, strewn across a

According to Aboriginal lore, the Devils Marbles are the eggs of the Rainbow Serpent.

wide, shallow valley. Many of the rocks balance precariously, looking as though they would topple at the slightest touch. The boulders are geological aberrations in a region otherwise worn flat by wind, rain and floods. They were originally part of a granite intrusion that formed underground. Once exposed by erosion, its surface cracked and crumbled into small pieces which were then worn into the smooth, rounded forms we see today. For local Aboriginal people, the rocks are the eggs of the Rainbow Serpent. Allow at least two hours to scramble among them.

On Stuart Hwy, 400 km north of the Alice. Parking. Toilets. Picnic tables. Wheelchair access. Caravans. Camping. ☎ 08-8951 8211.

The Gemtree ❾

This commercial set-up in what seems like the middle of nowhere has earned a place on the map by becoming a mecca for fossickers. The gem fields are located at **The Mud Tank Zircon Field**, about 17 km to the south-east. Visitors can enjoy a lesson in fossicking there, then, if lucky enough to find some precious stones, have them cut and polished at The Gemtree.

On Plenty Hwy, 137 km northeast of the Alice (69 km from Stuart Hwy). Open daily, 8 a.m.–6 p.m. Parking. Toilets. Kiosk. Picnic tables. BBQ. Limited store. Fuel. Cabins. Caravans (on-site vans). Camping. Fossicking tours and permits. Bookings essential for fossicking tours and accommodation. ☎ 08-8956 9855.

Native Gap Conservation Reserve ⑩

The Stuart Highway was built here over what explorer William Gosse referred to as "the native well" in his 1873 diary. Today's travellers use the small reserve set among cypress pines on the south side of the Hann Range as a scenic picnic spot. It is a significant site for local Aboriginals, believed to be part of several snake Dreamings that have connections with a ridge across the northern half of the reserve and a gum at the eastern end.

On Stuart Hwy, 110 km north of Alice Springs. Parking. Toilets. Picnic tables. BBQ. ☎ *08-8951 8211.*

Ryan Well Historical Reserve ⑪

The owners of Glen Maggie station once charged drovers and horseback travellers to draw water from this well, which was built in 1899 and is one of 16 in the Red Centre sunk with pick and shovel by a government team led by Irishman Ned Ryan. Motor vehicles and machine-sunk bores eventually made the well redundant, but the stone and timber supports for the 45,000-litre storage tank and watering trough remain as memorials to a man who spent most of his working life opening up the Centre to European settlement. Across the road are the ruins of **Glen Maggie Homestead**, built in 1914 for Sam Nicker and his family. It was used as a telegraph office and store from 1921, but abandoned in 1935, testimony to the hardship of life in this lonely outpost. It now makes an interesting rest stop for passing travellers.

On Stuart Hwy, 125 km north of the Alice. Parking. No toilets. No facilities. ☎ *08-8951 8211.*

Sample the life of a mineral prospector on one of the Gemtree's fossicking trips.

ROAD TRAINS

They're spectacular as they stir up a storm of red dust; they're also deadly dangerous to those who don't treat them with respect. Road trains have been a symbol of the Red Centre since the 1934 AEC truck, now in the Road Transport Hall of Fame in Alice Springs, first hitched up its trailer and in so doing replaced the overlanding drovers who walked cattle to distant markets. Often with three trailers and up to 50 m long, a single road train can carry 150 bullocks or up to 300 weaners. Many people pull over and stop when a road train approaches or wants to overtake in dusty conditions. Allow at least 1 km of clear road ahead before attempting to overtake one.

Ti Tree Roadhouse ⑫

You can cool off in the swimming pool or enjoy a Chinese meal at this well-known fuel stop on The Track. There are two art galleries in the tiny town and the roadhouse also sells Aboriginal art.

On Stuart Hwy, 193 km north of Alice Springs. Open daily, 6 a.m.–10 p.m. (limited service Christmas Day). Parking. Toilets. Restaurant/cafe. Picnic tables. BBQ. Store. Fuel. ☎ *08-8956 9741.*

Wauchope ⑬

To avoid sounding like strangers, readers should note that the name of this truckstop with a population of seven (plus camels, kangaroos and a donkey) is pronounced "war cup". The settlement is close to the Devils Marbles Conservation Reserve and has a swimming pool. Wolfram discovered nearby in 1917 was used in World War II munitions, and the hotel was built to serve the miners.

On Stuart Hwy, 390 km north of the Alice. Wauchope Hotel open daily, 6 a.m.–10 p.m. Parking. Toilets. Wheelchair access. Motel rooms. Caravans. Camping. Restaurant/cafe. Basic store. Fuel. ☎ 08-8964 1963.

Wycliffe Well ⑭

If you've always doubted the presence of UFOs in our skies, check the murals of them on the buildings here. Wycliffe Well is claimed to be one of the world's prime UFO-spotting sites. Before a night of spotting, pull a meal of redclaw or silver perch out of Lake Wycliffe and take in the nightly country-and-western show. Wycliffe Well, an important stockwatering point in the 1860s and again during construction of the Overland Telegraph Line, boasts an indoor swimming pool and animal sanctuary.

On Stuart Hwy, 372 km north of the Alice. Open 6.30 a.m.– 9 p.m. Parking. Toilets. Wheelchair access. Restaurant/cafe. Picnic tables. BBQ. Store. EFTPOS. Fuel. Motel. Caravans. Camping. ☎ 08-8964 1966.

Just a few of the exotic tourists reputed to have paid a visit to Wycliffe Well.

Fuel and a well-stocked store make Wauchope a handy pitstop on the Stuart Highway.

152 THE RED CENTRE

FURTHER AFIELD

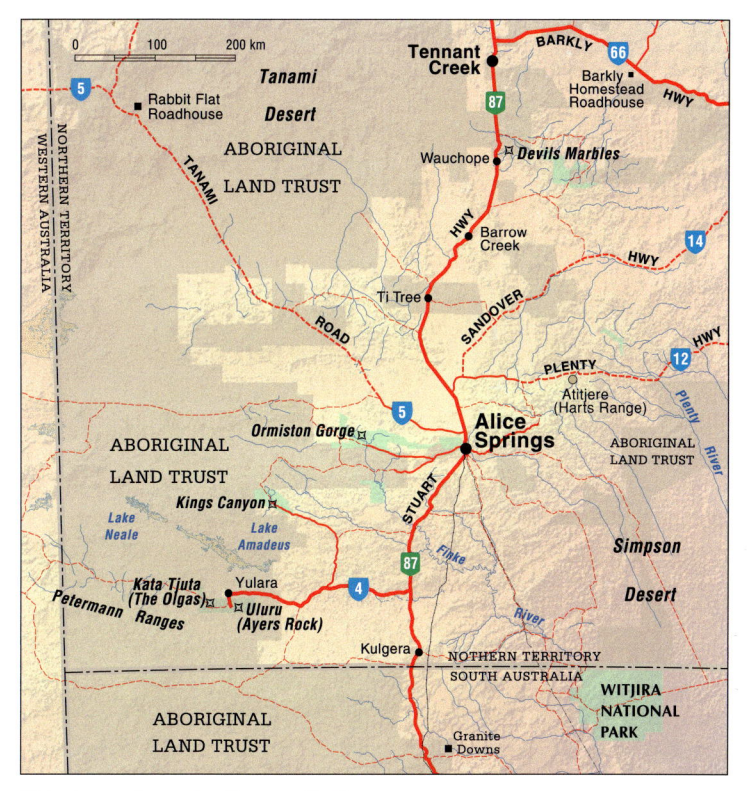

This sign on the road to Tennant Creek helps travellers get their bearings.

Further Afield

Harts Range Area ❶

Turning off the Stuart Highway and onto the Plenty Highway, about 68 km north of Alice Springs, travellers enter the Harts Range and its fossicking areas. For many years, these were among the most productive mineral sources in Australia for those dedicated enough to endure the tough, waterless conditions. Mica was discovered here in the 1890s, but its importance declined after World War II, when substitutes were found. Quartz, beryl, garnet, moonstone, prehnite, tourmaline and zircon are among the other gems and minerals found here. The mountains rise sharply from their surroundings to the south of the highway and boast a grandeur and colour variation to equal the MacDonnell Ranges. Mt Palmer (1136 m) is the highest point.

Harts Range (Atitjere) Store ❷

This Aboriginal community store is a handy supply post for fossickers heading deeper into the Harts Range, or travellers to and from Queensland. It has a small camping ground (no permit required) and a police station.

213 km north-east of the Alice (1 km south of Plenty Hwy). Open Monday–Friday, 9 a.m.–midday, 3 p.m.–5 p.m.; Saturday, 9 a.m.–midday. Parking. Toilets. Wheelchair access. Kiosk. Store. Fuel. Caravans and camping nearby. Store ☎ 08-8956 9773; police ☎ 08-8956 9772.

Plenty Highway ❸

In a landscape sometimes hauntingly beautiful, with shady stands of river gums and quirky ranges to explore, this shortcut to the Red Centre from the east includes sections of seemingly endless plain. Not that you'll really notice, while contending with the bulldust and corrugations, particularly on the Queensland side, where the route begins or ends at Boulia. With few facilities, limited fuel supplies and a sometimes daunting sense of isolation for almost its entire length, the Plenty Highway is not

Abandoned gold mines still dot the landscape around Tennant Creek.

Further Afield 155

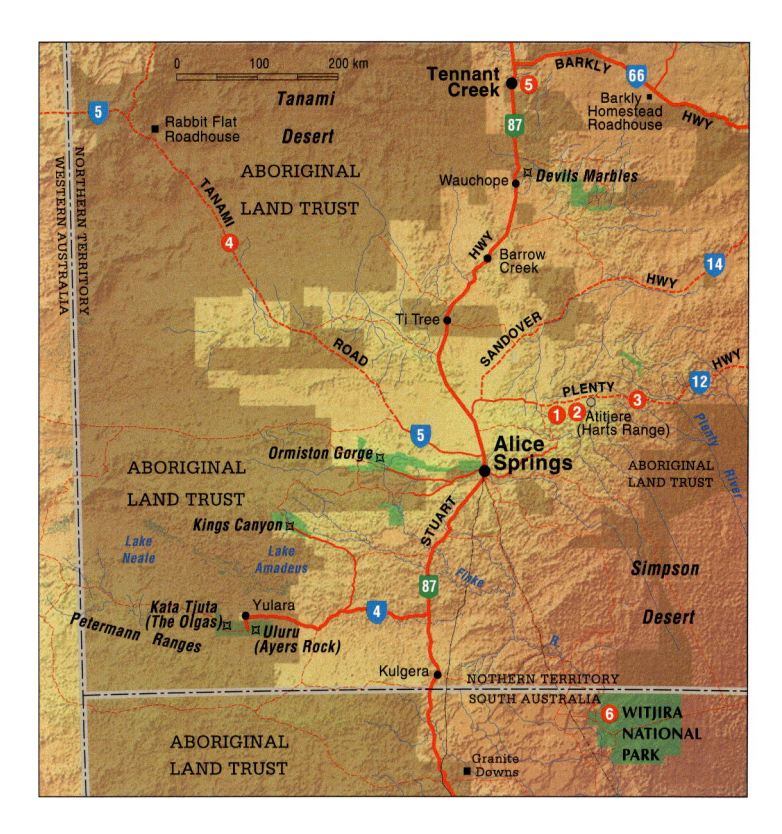

for the faint-hearted. But its directness and attractive sections, particularly around Harts Range (see North of Alice Springs, p. 142), are strong incentives for the adventurous and those who love to get away from it all. Another alternative to the Barkly Highway to and from Queensland is the Sandover Highway, which leaves the Plenty Highway soon after its junction with the Stuart Highway and leads to Lake Nash station, near the Queensland border. From there, the route to or from Mount Isa and other western Queensland destinations is by minor, unsealed roads.

Tanami Track ❹

This once-daunting route through the Tanami Desert has had many names, including Tragedy Track, which derives from the prospectors who perished humping their blueys or pushing their barrows to the fabled Tanami goldfields. Officially, it's the Tanami Road on the Northern Territory side and McGuire's Track on the Western Australia side. To the thousands who now travel its generally gentle surface each year, it's all the Tanami Track – a scenic 1040 km means of extending a trip to the Red Centre to take in the Kimberley and Top End. Mainly passing

Water pools at the centre of Wolfe Creek Meteorite Crater, supporting dense vegetation.

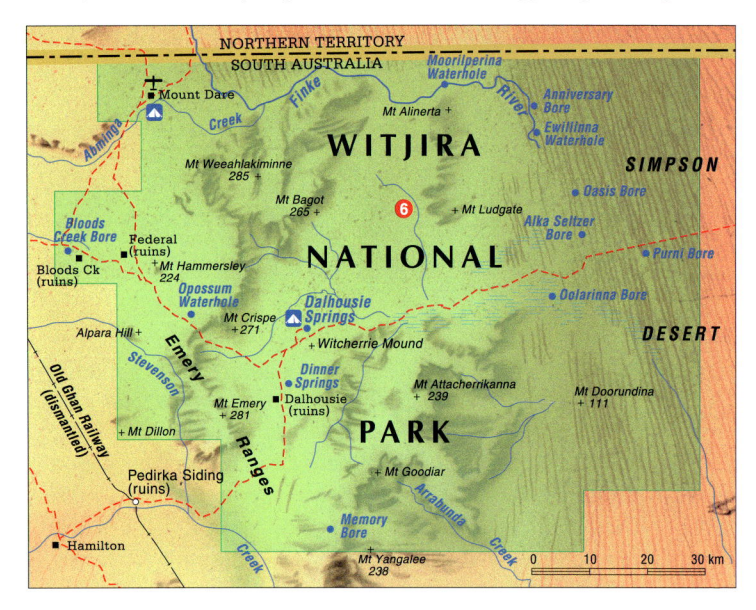

through flat, spinifex country with millions of termite mounds, it recommends itself as one of the least populated parts of Australia. Although the track is open to all, most of the land surrounding it is Aboriginal or under private lease, and entry is forbidden without permission. The Rabbit Flat Roadhouse is an important fuel stop, but travellers should check its opening times. One of the few tracks open to visitors goes to the region's main attraction – Wolfe Creek Meteorite Crater, the second largest in the world.

Further Afield 157

> ### TENNANT CREEK FACT FILE
>
> **Elevation:** 350 m
> **Population:** 4000
> **Location:** Tennant Creek is on the Stuart Highway, 504 km north of Alice Springs and 972 km south of Darwin. There are daily flights to the Alice (70 minutes; $216 one way) and Darwin (2 hours, 40 minutes; $336 one way), and regular coach services to the Alice (6 hours; $78 one way) and Darwin (13 hours, 40 minutes; $101 one way).
> **Police:** ☎ 08-8962 4444
> **Fire:** ☎ 08-8962 4577
> **Hospital:** Schmidt St; ☎ 08-8962 4399
> **Road service:** ☎ 08-8952 1087
> **Wildlife rescue:** ☎ 08-8962 4599
> **Visitor Information Centre:** Battery Hill, Peko Road, open daily May–September, 9 a.m.–5 p.m., October–April, Monday–Friday, 9 a.m.–5 p.m., Saturday 9 a.m.–midday; ☎ 08-8962 3388.
> **Taxi:** ☎ 08-8962 1061.

Tennant Creek ❺

Tennant Creek is the only major town between Alice Springs and Katherine, and for people travelling from the north on the Stuart Highway or from Queensland on the Barkly Highway, it is the gateway to the Red Centre. The settlement grew up around an important repeater station for the Overland Telegraph, its population swelling when thousands joined Australia's last gold rush in the 1930s. Today, Tennant Creek is the carefully preserved service centre of a busy region with many tourist attractions, including the telegraph station, goldmine tours, fossicking, station stays and bush camps. The Battery Hill Regional Centre overlooking the town has displays, films, a nature walk and tours of the working 10-stamp battery and underground mine. Its picnic area is popular for viewing the nearby ranges at sunset. Tennant Creek is also a handy base for exploring the Devils Marbles, an hour south of the town, and the proposed Davenport Range National Park (see North of Alice Springs).

Witjira National Park ❻

Outback enthusiasts seeking a multifaceted wilderness experience should head southeast from Alice Springs to Witjira National Park in northern South Australia, where the Finke River empties its floodwaters on the western edge of the Simpson Desert. The park includes the former Mt Dare cattle station (see Simpson Desert Loop in South-east of Alice) and Dalhousie Springs, which served as a base camp for many desert crossings, both in the days of early exploration and more recently. The springs, whose artesian water is more than 1 million years old, are of great biological and geological importance, as well as being a magnet for weary travellers. Other mound springs are found further south, notably along the

Backroads travellers seek advice from a local resident near Tennant Creek.

Oodnadatta Track, which also provides access to the park. Witjira's arid-zone landscape includes sand dunes, rolling gibber downs, dense coolibah woodlands and dissected plateaus known as "breakaways", with eroded gullies and flat hilltops, reminiscent of the scenery in B-grade Westerns. There are several established camping sites as well as designated bush-camping areas. On its eastern side, the park borders the enormous Simpson Desert Regional Reserve.

Built around 1885, Dalhousie homestead has often been used as a base by explorers.

Further Afield 159

Dalhousie's springs form a verdant oasis in a vast expanse of arid scrub.

160 *The Red Centre*

Suggested Tours

One-day Tour: East
MacDonnell Ranges		**162**

Two-day Tour: West
MacDonnell Ranges		**164**

Multi-day Tour: Yulara
and Kings Canyon		**166**

Whipping up red dust, a 4WD wends its way across the plains at day's end.

Suggested Tours

1. One-day tour: East MacDonnell Ranges

The major sites of the East MacDonnells lie within easy reach of Alice Springs. Some can only be reached by 4WD vehicles, but those described in the tour below are all accessible to conventional vehicles.

Head out to the East Macs via Ross Highway (State Highway 8), which branches off from the Stuart Highway at the southern end of Alice Springs. The sealed surface turns to gravel after about 70 km. A few kilometres further on, turn left towards Trephina Gorge Nature Park, which many visitors regard as the jewel of the region. The semi-permanent waterhole is a great place to relax and observe the many bird species that come here to drink, as well as the black-footed rock-wallabies that live among the red quartzite rocks surrounding the hole, the park also offers many fine walks.

If lunch is imminent, return to Ross Highway and continue eastwards. After about 5 km you will see the turn-off to Ross River Homestead, which is another 7 km off the road. The homestead is renowned for its hospitality, and the bar is a good spot to meet people who actually live in the area. You can also go camel riding here.

But make sure you leave time to visit Arltunga Historical Reserve, another 40 km to the east along

Ghost gums and river red gums flank the delightful waterhole at Trephina Gorge.

Travellers can mix with the locals in the bar at the Ross River Homestead.

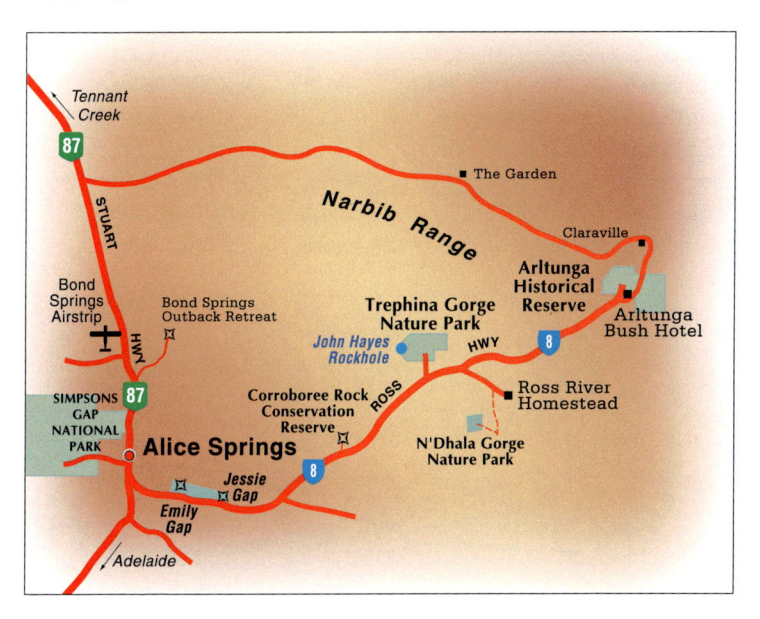

Ross Highway. Originally built by miners, this fascinating ghost town was the first European settlement in the Red Centre. If you want to hunt for gems, which is prohibited in the Historical Reserve, obtain a permit from the Arltunga Bush Hotel and head for the nearby fossicking reserve.

Return to Alice Springs along the Ross Highway. This shouldn't take you more than an hour-and-a-half, but beware of wildlife if you have to drive after nightfall.

2. Two-day tour: West MacDonnell Ranges

There is so much to see in the West MacDonnells that you could easily extend this tour by several days if you wish. However, accommodation options are limited unless you have a caravan or are prepared to camp. The sites described below can all be reached via sealed roads.

If you're heading south through Alice Springs, keep an eye out for Larapinta Drive (State Highway 6) near the southern end of town. Take this road and after 46 km turn right onto Namatjira Drive, in the direction of Glen Helen. About 90 km from the Alice is Ellery Creek Big Hole, a pleasant waterhole shaded by river red gums. There is a fascinating 3 km walk with signs that explain how to interpret the geological features in the surrounding rocks.

Serpentine Gorge, with its string of waterholes, lies 11 km farther along Namatjira Drive, and 8 km beyond it are the colourful Ochre Pits which continue to be mined by Aboriginal people for pigments used in their art and ceremonies. The 4 km nature track from the Ochre Pits to Inarlanga Pass is well worth the effort; alternatively, you can work your legs a bit harder on the Larapinta Trail, which passes at this point.

Returning to the main road, continue on until you reach Glen Helen Gorge, 22 km to the west. This huge permanent waterhole is an oasis in the middle of a desert,

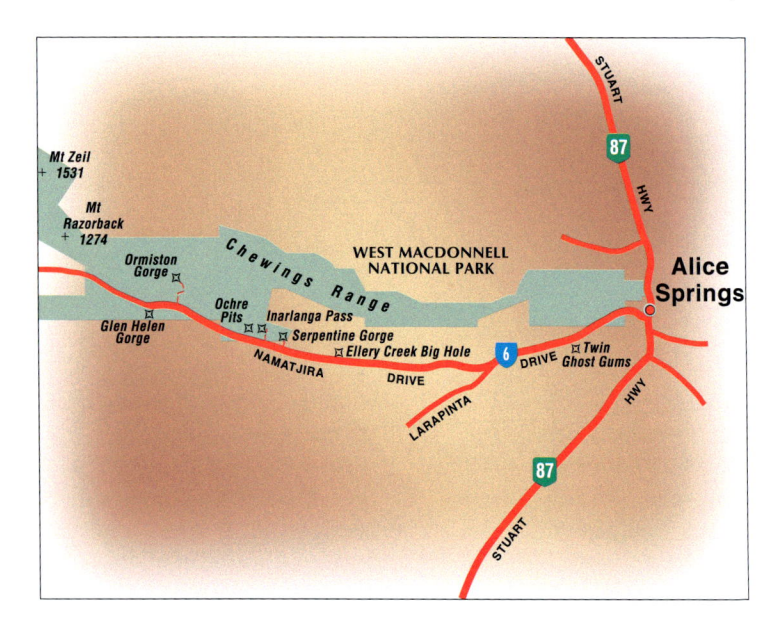

The precipitous sandstone cliffs of Glen Helen Gorge glow red in the setting sun.

cool, shady and picturesque, it draws wildlife and visitors from all around. The old station homestead at the gorge offers the only restaurant, bar and accommodation to be found in the area; you can also camp here, or head 4 km back along the road and camp at Ormiston Gorge.

Whatever you choose to do, Ormiston Gorge deserves a leisurely visit. The waterhole, surrounded by gums, is a perfect place to cool down on hot days; there are also an informative ranger station and several grades of walks. The 300 m cliffs of the gorge are particularly dramatic, not least because they change colour throughout the day as the sun passes overhead. And if you sit quietly in the gorge in the late afternoon, you may find a black-footed rock-wallaby appearing suddenly beside you.

When the sun is high, spinifex pigeons rest on the ground in shallow hollows.

Return to Alice Springs along Namatjira Drive. Watch for the various lookout points that are signposted along the way, many of which provide spectacular views of the entire range. You can also pause, if there's time around sunset, at the viewpoint for the twin ghost gums made famous by Aboriginal artist Albert Namatjira, 19 km before Alice Springs.

3. Multi-day tour: Yulara and Kings Canyon

This multi-day trip takes in the three classic destinations of the Red Centre – Uluru, Kata Tjuta and Kings Canyon (Watarrka) – all of which can be reached by sealed roads. An optional extension leads back to Alice Springs via the unsealed Mereenie Loop Road. Travellers in conventional vehicles should only attempt this when road and weather conditions are favourable. Those planning to take the Mereenie Loop Road must carry a permit that allows them to cross Aboriginal land. This can be obtained from the Central Land Council in Alice Springs before departure.

From Alice Springs, head south along the Stuart Highway (National Highway 87) in the direction of Adelaide. About 90 km from the Alice you'll come to Stuart's Well where you will find Jim's Place, a roadhouse run by the Cotterill family, pioneers of tourism in the Red Centre. The roadhouse is decorated with interesting photographs and other memorabilia, and is a good place to stop for a chat about the history of the area. A little further down the road you'll find Camel Outback Safaris, where you can take a trip back in time by going on a camel safari. The company offers excursions lasting minutes, hours or even days.

Continuing on down the Stuart Highway, you will see the turn-off to Henbury Meteorites Conservation Reserve on the right, some 55 km beyond Jim's

Swap your car for a camel and sample outback travel as it was a century ago.

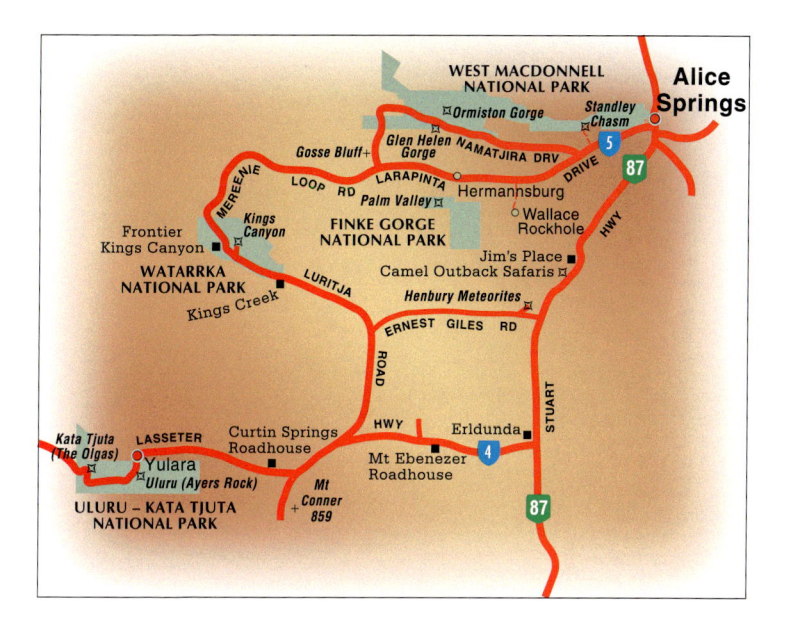

Place. You need to drive for 11 km along a gravel road (Ernest Giles Road), and look out for the reserve on your right. There are 12 meteorite craters here, of which the largest is 180 m wide and 15 m deep. The terrain is said to bear an uncanny resemblance to the surface of the Moon – so much so that US astronauts trained here in preparation for their lunar landings. There are limited facilities, and camping is allowed.

Return to the Stuart Highway and continue south to Erldunda – also known as the Desert Oaks Motel – which lies about half-way to Yulara and has a service station, store, tavern and a wide range of accommodation. If you've been stopping along the way from the Alice, you may want to pause overnight here before continuing to Yulara, which lies 240 km to the west, at the end of the Lasseter Highway (State Highway 4).

Alternatively, you could push on to Mount Ebenezer Roadhouse, 65 km further on, which has accommodation as well as a

Sealed roads lead to most major sites.

At Wallace Rockhole, local guides offer tours to visit the area's superb rock art.

gallery of Aboriginal paintings and artefacts produced by the nearby Impana community. Another place to consider is Curtin Springs station, 157 km from Erldunda, from where you can watch the setting sun light up the cliffs of Mt Conner. Day visitors can join tours of the station arranged at the station's roadhouse.

Continue on to Yulara, the resort serving the Uluru–Kata Tjuta National Park. All necessary facilities can be found here, including a medical centre, post office, supermarket and a range of other shops. Accommodation ranges from camping through backpackers to a five-star hotel with swimming pool. You should allow two days to see both Uluru and Kata Tjuta – the latter situated 51 km from Yulara. Camping is not permitted in the park, so you have to return to Yulara every night. But don't rush back too early: both Uluru and Kata Tjuta have their own viewing areas from where you can see the rocks dramatically change colour in the light of the setting sun.

Heading on to Kings Canyon in Watarrka National Park, you need to drive back along the Lasseter Highway in the direction of Erldunda, but turn off to the left approximately half way (133 km) from Yulara. Kings Canyon lies about 170 km from the turn-off, and is seen at its best in the early morning and evening. For this reason it is worth staying overnight, either at the Kings Canyon resort, or at Kings Creek Station 32 km to the east, just outside the park. Some walking tracks are short and easy, but others are distinctly arduous; determined hikers can head into distant gorges for a couple of days of solitude.

To return to Alice Springs, most travellers retrace their journey along the Lasseter and Stuart highways, but the more adventurous might be inclined to take the unsealed Mereenie Loop Road to Hermannsburg. Remember that it is essential to check on road conditions with the Kings Canyon park ranger before attempting this route, and also to have a permit allowing you to cross Aboriginal land. Overnight camping is not permitted along this road, which runs for about 170 km through magnificent, isolated terrain before joining Larapinta Drive, 33 km west of Hermannsburg Aboriginal community. The Kata Anga Tearoom at Hermannsburg offers a welcome break after the arduous drive along the Mereenie Road, and the Hermannsburg Historic Precinct is well worth a visit. Some 36 km further east is the turn-off to Wallace Rockhole, another Aboriginal community with a thriving arts and crafts centre. Tours of the rockhole led by local guides explain Aboriginal beliefs and the meanings of the petroglyphs that are found there.

Larapinta Drive will take you straight back to the Alice, but along the way you can take a side-trip to dramatic Standley Chasm – which should be visited at midday, when the sun overhead lights up the interior of the deep gorge – and pause at the viewpoint facing the twin ghost gums associated with artist Albert Namatjira.

The ragged ridges of the George Gill Range rise north-west of Kings Canyon.

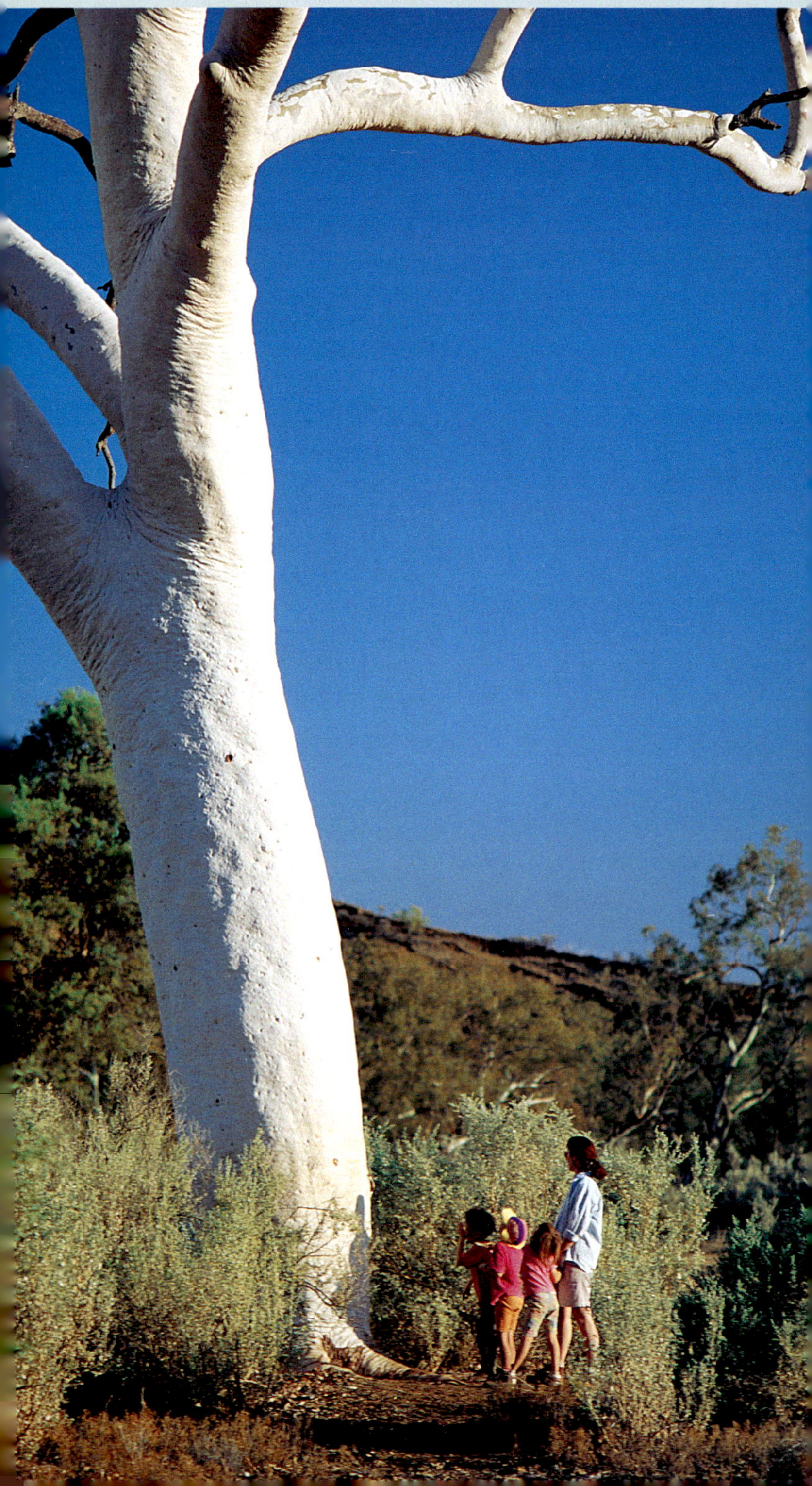

Reference Directory

This 33 m tall ghost gum at Trephina Gorge is one of the region's largest.

REFERENCE DIRECTORY

Old Andado station occupies a shallow valley amid the desert's red dunes.

Information Centres

Central Australian Tourism Industry Association (CATIA), 60 Gregory Tce, Alice Springs NT 0870, ☎ 08-8952 5800.

Tennant Creek Regional Tourist Association, Battery Hill Information Centre, Peko Rd, Tennant Creek NT 0860, ☎ 08-8962 3388.

Ayers Rock Resort Visitors Centre, Ayers Rock Resort, Yulara, ☎ 08-8957 7377.

Ayers Rock Resort Tour and Information Centre, Shopping Centre, Ayers Rock Resort, Yulara, ☎ 08-8956 2240.

Northern Territory Tourist Commission, 67 North Stuart Hwy, Alice Springs, ☎ 08-8951 8555; Holiday Centre for tour and travel information and bookings, ☎ 1800 621 336.

Parks and Wildlife Commission of the Northern Territory, Arid Zone Research Institute, Tom Hare Building, South Stuart Hwy, Alice Springs, ☎ 08-8951 8211.

Attractions

Uluru–Kata Tjuta Cultural Centre, ☎ 08-8956 3138, provides a valuable introduction to this World Heritage area and the lifestyle and beliefs of its traditional owners.

Arltunga Historical Reserve, 110 km east of Alice Springs, ☎ 08-8951 8211, encompasses restored buildings, stone ruins and the scattered workings of a former gold-mining town.

Old Andado Homestead, 330 km south-east of Alice Springs, ☎ 08-8956 0812, is Molly Clark's legendary open-house on the edge of the Simpson Desert. Advance bookings are essential.

In Alice Springs:

The Alice Springs Cultural Precinct, ☎ 08-8951 1120, incorporates the Araluen Centre for Arts and Entertainment, the Central Australian Aviation Museum, the Memorial Cemetery, the Museum of Central Australia and Territory Craft.

The Alice Springs Telegraph Station Historical Reserve, ☎ 08-8952 3993, features beautifully restored buildings that are the remnants of the town's first European settlement.

The Royal Flying Doctor Visitor Centre, ☎ 08-8952 1129, explains how the RFDS has been providing a "mantle of safety" to far-flung families since 1939.

The School of the Air, ☎ 08-8951 6834, is the on-air classroom for students as far as 1000 km away.

The Transport Heritage Centre, 10 km south of Alice Springs, combines the Old Ghan Train, ☎ 08-8955 5047, and the Road Transport Hall of Fame, ☎ 08-8952 7161.

Main Parks and Reserves

Alice Springs Desert Park, Larapinta Drive, ☎ 08-8951 8788, provides an excellent introduction to the habitats, flora and fauna of the Red Centre.

Olive Pink Botanic Garden, Tuncks Rd, Alice Springs, ☎ 08-8952 2154.

West MacDonnell National Park ranger stations are located at Simpsons Gap, ☎ 08-8955 0310, and Ormiston Gorge, ☎ 08-8956 7799.

The sites in the **East MacDonnell Ranges**, the **Devils Marbles Conservation Reserve** and the sites in the region south-east of Alice Springs **Ewaninga Rock Carvings Conservation Reserve**, **Rainbow Valley Conservation Reserve**, **Chambers Pillar Historical Reserve and Mac Clark Conservation Reserve** are administered by the Parks and Wildlife Commission of the Northern Territory, ☎ 08-8951 8211.

Finke Gorge National Park ranger station, ☎ 08-8956 7401.

Information on **Uluru–Kata Tjuta National Park** is available from the Uluru–Kata Tjuta Cultural Centre, ☎ 08-8956 3138.

Watarrka National Park ranger station, ☎ 08-8956 7488.

The proposed Davenport Range National Park has no ranger station but information is available from the adjoining property, Kurundi station, ☎ 08-8964 1964.

The Desert Parks District, ☎ 08-8648 5300 or 1800 816 078, covers Witjira, Simpson Desert Conservation Park, Simpson Desert Regional Reserve, Innamincka Regional Reserve, Lake Eyre, Elliot Price Conservation Park, Tallaringa Conservation Park, Wabma Kadarbu Conservation Park and Strzelecki Regional Reserve.

Key Bushwalks

West MacDonnells:

Section One of the Larapinta Trail is a 23.7 km trek; there is a camping ground at Wallaby Gap.

The Woodland Walk from Simpsons Gap to Bond Gap is 8 km each way.

The Nature Trail from the Ochre Pits to the cycad-studded, ceremonially significant Inarlanga Pass is 4 km each way.

It's a 7 km loop from Ormiston Gorge to the 10 km diameter Ormiston Pound. From Redbank Gorge to the summit of Mt Sonder is a tough 8 km walk each way.

Palm Valley:

The Mpaara Track is a 5 km circuit that explains local Dreamings and offers views of the cliffs of Kalarranga.

The 5 km circuit of the Mpulungkinya Track takes walkers from Palm Valley to the arid plateau above.

East MacDonnells:

Trephina Gorge has five tracks ranging in length from 1.2 to 18 km.

It's a scenic 8 km along the ridge from Emily Gap to Jessie Gap.

Watarrka National Park:

The Kings Canyon (Rim) Walk is a 6 km circuit that reveals the majesty of this extraordinary rock formation.

The Giles Track is a 22 km overnight trek from Kathleen Springs to Kings Canyon.

Uluru–Kata Tjuta National Park:

The Uluru Base Walk is a gentle 9.4 km track around the perimeter of the Rock.

The wheelchair-accessible Mala Walk to Kantju Gorge is 2 km each way.

The Valley of the Winds Walk is a 7.4 km circuit taking in Karu and Karingana lookouts.

The Walpa or Olga Gorge Walk is an easy 2.6 km walk each way.

Key Tourist Drives

The Ross River Highway takes in the gorges of the East MacDonnells including Trephina and Emily and Jessie gaps, the Ross River Homestead and Arltunga.

Larapinta Drive takes in John Flynn's Grave, Simpsons Gap and Standley Chasm before heading south-west to Wallace Rockhole, Hermannsburg and Finke Gorge National Park (4WD access only). It eventually connects to the Mereenie Loop Road (permit required), which provides unsealed access to Kings Canyon (Watarrka NP). This road is not suitable for conventional vehicles, and travellers should check the road conditions locally before setting out on their journey.

Namatjira Drive heads west of the Alice through the West MacDonnell NP, providing access to Ellery Creek Big Hole, Serpentine Gorge, the Ochre Pits and Ormiston, Glen Helen and Redbank gorges.

The Finke River 4WD Route provides 4WD-only access from Finke Gorge National Park to Ernest Giles Road.

The Simpson Desert Loop is a 4WD-only, 970 km loop south-east of Alice Springs taking in attractions including the Ewaninga Rock Carvings, Chambers Pillar, Rainbow

Valley, Mac Clark Conservation Reserve and Old Andado Homestead.

The Stuart Highway, better known as The Track, is the main highway between Adelaide and Darwin, and Alice Springs is the mid-point on this journey of approximately 3000 km. About 200 km south of Alice Springs the highway connects to the Lasseter Highway which leads to Yulara and Uluru–Kata Tjuta NP. This highway in turn connects to the sealed Luritja Road to Watarrka NP.

Permits and Passes

For permits to visit Aboriginal land and communities, contact the Central Land Council, 33 Stuart Hwy, Alice Springs 0871, ☎ 08-8951 6320.

Fossicking permits are available from Minerals House, 58 Hartley St, Alice Springs, ☎ 08-8951 5658; the CATIA office, 60 Gregory Tce, Alice Springs, ☎ 08-8952 5800; Arltunga Bush Hotel, Arltunga Tourist Drive, Arltunga, ☎ 08-8956 9797; The Gemtree Caravan Park, Plenty Hwy, The Gemtree, ☎ 08-8956 9855 and Tennant Creek Regional Tourist Association, Battery Hill Regional Centre, Peko Rd, Tennant Creek, ☎ 08-8962 3388.

The Uluru–Kata Tjuta NP entrance station, ☎ 08-8956 2252, sells a $15 entry pass for adults, valid for three days. Children under 16 years enter free.

A **Desert Parks Pass** is required for nine parks and reserves in the far north of South Australia ($60 for a year). The pass covers Witjira NP, Simpson Desert Conservation Park, Simpson Desert Regional Reserve, Innamincka Regional Reserve, Lake Eyre NP, Elliot Price Conservation Park, Tallaringa Conservation Park, Wabma Kadarbu Conservation Park and Strzelecki Regional Reserve and is managed by the South Australian Department for Environment, Heritage and Aboriginal Affairs, 9 Mackay St, Port Augusta SA 5700, ☎ 08-8648 5300 or 1800 816 078.

Festivals/Events

APRIL/MAY

During **Heritage Week** the residents of Alice Springs participate in a wide range of activities coordinated by the National Trust and aimed at promoting greater appreciation of the Red Centre's rich history. Groups including the Alice Springs Town Council and the Parks and Wildlife Commission of the Northern Territory organise a host of re-enactments, camel and horse police patrols, displays, open houses at heritage properties, historic walks and talks and a film evening at the old Pioneer Walk-in theatre. Information: Bev Ayres, ☎ 08-8952 4516.

The Alice Springs Cup Carnival features a month of horseracing meetings held at Pioneer Park, culminating in The Cup, which takes place on the first Monday in

Alice Springs Desert Park plays a vital role in rehabilitating injured wildlife.

Outback hospitality can be sampled at a wide range of establishments.

May, and a black-tie ball on the lawns of Lasseters Hotel Casino. Information: Stephen Smedley, ☎ 08-8952 4977.

MAY

The Bangtail Muster commemorates Central Australia's long connection with the cattle industry. In bygone days, stockmen would record the number of cattle mustered by cutting off the hair at the end of their tails. Today's muster consists of a parade of floats followed by a sports afternoon. It is usually held on the first Monday in May, which is a public holiday in the Alice and coincides with the Alice Springs Cup. Information: Secretary, Rotary Club of Alice Springs, ☎ 08-8955 0252.

Molly's Bash is an annual Mother's Day event organised by Molly Clark of the Old Andado Homestead to raise funds for the National Pioneer Women's Hall of Fame. Entertainment under the stars is the highlight of the weekend, which is held at Old Andado Station, 330 km south-east of the Alice. Camping facilities, a bar and meals are available. Information: Molly Clark, ☎ 08-8956 0812.

The Tennant Creek Cup is an annual horseracing meeting held at Hagan Park with live entertainment in the evening. Information: Greg Targett, ☎ 08-8962 2006.

The streets of Tennant Creek come alive during the **Australian Street Circuit Go-Kart Grand Prix**, held during the first weekend in May. The event attracts local, national and international competitors of all ages as well as enthusiastic spectators from near and far. Information: Jack Gannon, ☎ 08-8962 3007 or 0419 851 229.

JUNE

The Finke Desert Race is a gruelling 460 km return off-road event for cars and motorcycles held each year on the Queen's birthday long weekend. The challenge is not so much to win, but simply to complete the course to Aputula and back to the Alice. Competitors come from the Centre, other parts of Australia and overseas. Information: Finke Desert Race Office, ☎ 08-8952 8886.

JULY

The Alice Springs Show is a two-day agricultural and horticultural show held at Blatherskite Park. Attractions include ring events, a sideshow alley and a spectacular fireworks display. Information: Lyn Oliver, ☎ 08-8952 1651.

The Tennant and Districts Show at Jubilee Park combines an agricultural show with rock-drilling championships and equestrian events. Information: Tony Boulter, ☎ 08-8962 2791.

The Lions Camel Cup Carnival is an annual Alice Springs charity fundraiser culminating in camel races and including a pocamelo (polo on camels) match in the rodeo ring. Information: Bill O'Flaherty, ☎ 08-853 2300.

AUGUST

The Harts Range Annual Races are a traditional bush meeting held each year at the Harts Range race track, 200 km north-east of the Alice, on the first weekend of August. Horseracing is supported by a family sports day with lizard-racing and bull tail-throwing, a ball and bush dance. Information: Gillian Furniss, ☎ 0418 816 361.

Bush racing, a gymkhana and sports events make the **Barrow Creek Races** near historic Barrow Creek Telegraph Station, 284 km north of Alice Springs, an entertaining family day out. Information: Louise Binder, ☎ 08-8956 9756.

Events at the **Alice Springs Rodeo** include saddle and bareback bronco, bull-riding, calf-roping, steer-wrestling and barrel-racing. Cowboys and cowgirls from all over Australia compete for top prize money at Blatherskite Park. Information: Ron Woodall, ☎ 03-5528 4224.

SEPTEMBER

The Great Pram Battle is an eccentric relay run that begins at the the Yulara Town Oval. Teams of four runners push a "baby" (aged over 18) around the resort's ring-road to raise money for charity. Information: Tamie Brand, ☎ 08-8956 2097.

OCTOBER

The Rydges Henley-on Todd Regatta is Alice Springs' famous waterless boating competition. The combined Rotary clubs of the town organise a range of madcap races in bottomless boats along the dry bed of the Todd River. These include warship battles and events for rowing eights, boogie boards and yachts. Information: Bill van Dijk, ☎ 08-8955 1253.

The Alice Springs Food and Wine Festival, held at Chateau Hornsby, showcases the talents of local restaurateurs and winemakers from further afield. Information: Denis Hornsby, ☎ 08-8955 5133.

OCTOBER/NOVEMBER

The Alice Prize Art Exhibition is an exhibition of works entered for this national contemporary art award, which is judged by Australia's leading museum directors. The skills of about 60 Australian artists, sculptors and photographers are displayed at the Araluen Cultural Precinct, and all works are for sale. Information: Patricia van Dijk, ☎ 08-8955 0252.

NOVEMBER

The Corkwood Festival is organised by Territory Craft and the Folk Society of Alice Springs. Held annually on the last Sunday in November at Anzac Oval, this entertaining festival is a celebration of local art, craft, music, entertainment and food, which concludes with a lively bush dance. Information: Martell Dunn or Karen Montey, ☎ 08-8952 4417.

DECEMBER

On New Year's Eve at **Chateau Hornsby**, the Northern Territory's only winery, a party is held to herald the start of vintage. Just a few minutes after midnight, shiraz grapes are picked and used to make what is claimed to be the world's first vintage of the new year. Information: Denis Hornsby, ☎ 08-8955 5133.

Aboriginal Arts and Crafts Galleries

Papunya Tula Artists, 78 Todd St, Alice Springs, ☎ 08-8952 4731.

Roslyn Premont, Gallery Gondwana Fine Art, Alice Springs, ☎ 08-8953 1577.

Maruku Arts and Crafts, Uluru–Kata Tjuta Cultural Centre, ☎ 08-8956 2558.

Aboriginal Art and Cultural Centre, 86 Todd St, Alice Springs, incorporates a museum, art gallery, cultural performance and even a didgeridoo "university" that guarantees to teach students how to get a good sound out of the instrument. It also provides tips on purchasing Aboriginal art as well as presenting a range of works for sale, ☎ 08-8952 3408.

Helen Read of Didgeri Air Art Tours, ☎ 08-8948 5055 or 0418 137 719, flies all the major dealers, serious art buyers and interested people to Aboriginal communities in the Territory. She operates by charter and arranges meetings with the artists, permits, accommodation, food, ground transport and all other aspects of the art tour.

Airlines

Qantas Travel Centre, cnr Todd Mall and Parsons St, Alice Springs, ☎ 08-8950 5211; bookings: ☎ 13 13 13.

Ansett Australia, Alice Springs Airport, ☎ 08-8950 4156; bookings: ☎ 13 13 00.

Coach Companies

McCafferty's Terminal, Shop 3, 91 Gregory Tce, Alice Springs, ☎ 08-8952 3952; bookings: ☎ 13 14 99.

Greyhound–Pioneer Terminal, Shop 22, Coles complex, Gregory Tce, Alice Springs, ☎ 08-8952 7888; bookings: ☎ 13 20 30.

Trains

Great Southern Railway, Burbridge Rd, Mile End, SA 5031. PO Box 668, Marleston Business Centre, Marleston, SA 5033. Bookings: ☎ 13 21 47.

Vehicle Hire

Hertz Northern Territory, 76 Hartley St, Alice Springs, ☎ 08-8952 2644; Touring and Information Centre, Yulara, ☎ 08-8956 2244.

Avis, 52 Hartley St, Alice Springs, ☎ 08-8953 5533; Connellan Airport, Uluru, ☎ 08-8956 2266.

Budget Rent A Car, 10 Gap Rd, Alice Springs, ☎ 08-8952 8899.

Camper and 4WD companies:

Outback Auto Rental, 78 Todd St, Alice Springs, ☎ 08-8953 5333.

Britz Australia Rentals, cnr Stuart Hwy and Power St, Alice Springs, ☎ 08-8952 8814.

Apollo Motorhome Holidays, 3 Larapinta Dr, Alice Springs, ☎ 08-8952 7255.

Contact the Northern Territory Department of Transport and Works Road Information Service, ☎ 1800 246 199, for up-to-date **road condition reports**. The national road service: ☎ 13 11 11.

Tour Operators

AAT Kings, 74 Todd St, Alice Springs, ☎ 08-8952 1700 or 1800 896 111; Touring and Information Centre, Ayers Rock Resort,

Yulara, ☎ 08-8956 2171. This leading coach company offers everything from sunrise and sunset tours of Uluru to comprehensive tours taking in the main attractions of the Red Centre.

Sahara Outback Tours, ☎ 08-8953 0881 or 1800 806 240, has a range of budget-priced camping tours from Alice to Uluru, the Olgas and Kings Canyon including a five-day safari that takes in Uluru, Kings Canyon, Wallace Rockhole, Palm Valley and the gorges of the West MacDonnells.

Australian Pacific Tours, ☎ 1800 675 222, is a coach company offering everything from day tours around Uluru and seven-day Red Centre packages to tours taking in all the attractions from Adelaide to the Top End.

Tailormade Tours, ☎ 08-8952 1731 or 1800 806 641; at Yulara, ☎ 08-8956 2195, offers personalised itineraries in luxury vehicles. Passengers are collected from their accommodation at Uluru and Alice Springs.

VIP Tours, ☎ 08-8956 2388 or 1800 806 412, provides coach and chauffeur-driven limo tours around Uluru, Kata Tjuta and Alice Springs.

Aerial Tours

Ayers Rock Helicopters, ☎ 08-8956 2077, fly over Uluru, Kata Tjuta, Lake Amadeus, landing on Mt Conner; they are also based at Kings Creek Station, near Watarrka, ☎ 08-8956 7474.

Professional Helicopter Services at Uluru, ☎ 08-8956 2003, offers scenic and charter flights over Uluru, Kata Tjuta, Lake Amadeus and Mt Conner; also based at Kings Canyon Resort, near Watarrka, and the Glen Helen Resort, ☎ 08-8956 7489.

Rockayer, ☎ 08-8956 2345, conducts fixed-wing flights over Uluru, Kata Tjuta, Lake Amadeus and to Kings Canyon with time to complete the Kings Canyon (Rim) walk and have lunch before returning to Yulara.

Outback Mail Flights with Ngurratjuta Air, ☎ 08-8953 5000.

Murray Cosson, ☎ 08-8952 4625 or 0419 804 386, runs an aerial charter service from Alice to anywhere.

Didgeri Air Art Tours, ☎ 08-8948 5055 or 0418 137 719.

Adventure and Special-Interest Tour Operators

Sahara Tours, ☎ 08-8953 0881 or 1800 806 240, offers a range of camping safaris in Central Australia for small groups, including charter tours.

Ian Barker's Station Tours, ☎ 08-8953 4664 or 08-8956 2906, for Curtin Springs and Mt Conner tours as well as daytrips from Alice Springs to Uluru.

The Ghan arrives in Alice Springs after its 19-hour journey from Adelaide.

Rise with the sun on a dawn balloon flight over the rockscapes of the Centre.

Experience Australia Ecotours, ☎ 08-8956 2563 or 1800 803 174, has both Yulara and Alice Springs operations.

Uluru Experience provides 4WD or minibus tours around attractions at Uluru and to Mt Conner and Curtin Springs cattle station. The signature tour is a guided dawn walk around the base of Uluru.

Alice Springs Experience has half- and full-day tours of the Alice and nearby attractions. The Eyes in the Dark tour combines a night walk and BBQ on the Todd River at Bond Springs station.

The Outback Experience's Simpson Desert Day Tour from Alice Springs provides a big day out in the desert in 4WD vehicles, taking in the Ewaninga rock carvings, Chambers Pillar and Rainbow Valley, ☎ 08-8953 2666.

Walking:

Jim's Bush Tours, ☎ 08-8952 5305 or 08-8953 1975, offers walking tours in the East and West Macs with Jim Cowie.

Trek Larapinta, ☎ 08-8953 2933, offers guided walks on the Larapinta Trail with biologist and anthropologist Dr Charlie Carter.

Overnight Walkers Registration Scheme, ☎ 1300 650 730. The scheme is designed to ensure the safety of walkers using tracks within national parks and is operated by the Parks and Wildlife Commission.

Hot-air ballooning:

Spinifex Ballooning, Shed 6, 70 Elder St, Alice Springs, ☎ 08-8953 4800 or 1800 677 893, for dawn flights with pick-up from all Alice accommodations.

Outback Ballooning, 35 Kennett Crt, Alice Springs, ☎ 08-8952 8723 or 1800 809 790, for dawn flights with pick-up from all Alice accommodations.

Horse-riding:

Ross River Homestead, Ross Highway, 85 km east of Alice, ☎ 08-8956 9711 or 1800 241 711, offers everything from a 10-minute led ride for children and two-hour treks, to overnight camping-out treks. Pick up from the Alice by arrangement.

Ooraminna Bush Camp, Deep Well station, 30 km south of the Alice, ☎ 08-8953 0170, has trail rides plus add-on choice of dinner and sleeping in swags under the stars with pick-up and return to the Alice.

Ossie's Outback Horse Tours, 18 Warburton St, Alice Springs, ☎ 08-8952 2308 or 1800 628 211, has three-hour nature treks, day, sunset, lunch and overnight camping-out tours.

Camel-riding:

Frontier Camel Tours, Ross Hwy, 4 km from Alice Springs, ☎ 08-8953 0444; Ayers Rock Resort, ☎ 08-8956 2444.

Camel Outback Safaris, Stuart Hwy, Stuarts Well, 90 km south of the Alice, ☎ 08-8956 0925.

Ross River Homestead, Ross Hwy, 85 km east of the Alice, near N'Dhala Gorge, ☎ 08-8956 9711 or 1800 241 711.

Kings Creek station, near Watarrka National Park, 35 km east of Kings Canyon, ☎ 08-8956 7474.

Cycling:

Steve's Mountain Bike Tours, 5/1 Kempe St, Alice Springs, ☎ 08-8952 1542, offers one- to five-hour off-road tours in the open desert country around Alice Springs for experienced mountain-bikers.

Motorbike tours:

High on the Hog Harley Adventures, ☎ 08-8953 4755, offers a wide range of excursions, from one-hour to full-day tours from Alice Springs to the East and West MacDonnell ranges.

Uluru Motor Cycle Tours, ☎ 08-8956 2019, offers passenger and self-ride outings around Uluru, Kata Tjuta and to Kings Canyon.

Aboriginal Culture

Anangu Tours, Ayers Rock Resort Tour and Information Centre, Shopping Centre, Ayers Rock Resort, Yulara, ☎ 08-8956 2123, offers Aboriginal-guided cultural tours departing from the Uluru–Kata Tjuta Cultural Centre.

Aboriginal Art and Culture Centre, Alice Springs, 86 Todd St, Alice Springs, ☎ 08-8952 3408, combines an art gallery, didgeridoo school and cultural performance space with a base for half- and full-day Aboriginal culture tours as well as extended tours to the Pwerte Marnte Marnte community near Rainbow Valley.

Didgeri Air Art Tours, PO Box 108, Parap, Darwin 0804, ☎ 08-8948 5055 or 0418 137 719, arranges visits to Aboriginal communities for serious art collectors.

Lilla Tours guides visitors through an area dotted with sacred caves and paintings at Lilla ("sweet-water rockhole") near Kings Canyon. The tours include talks on Aboriginal lore, bush tucker and the medicinal properties of native plants, and conclude with boomerang- and spear-throwing lessons. Bookings through Kings Canyon Resort, ☎ 08-8956 7442.

The Wallace Rockhole community, ☎ 08-8956 7993, welcomes visitors and accompanies them to a rock-art site featuring engravings and hand stencils. Groups of a minimum of four can follow the tour with a meal of billy tea, damper and kangaroo tail. There's a camping ground and cabin accommodation at the community.

Visual Arts and Specialist Tours, PO Box 2432, Alice Springs, NT 0871, ☎ 08-8952 8233, organises an art advisor to join charter flights for cultural tours and buying trips to remote Aboriginal communities.

182 THE RED CENTRE

INDEX

Hikers gather to watch the sunset from Kalarranga Lookout in Palm Valley.

Using this index:
Entries appearing in a caption only are set in *italics*. Regular or recurring festivals, celebrations, etc. are listed under Events. Individual locality maps are listed under Maps. An overview of a subject will be found in the general index under a broad heading, e.g. Central Australia, geology. Note that locality names may also refer to pastoral properties. Some widely known Aboriginal communities, e.g. Hermannsburg, are listed in the general index.

Aboriginal Art and Culture Centre, *14*, 56
Aboriginal lands, travel permits, 47, 175
Aboriginal-led tours, 118, 119–20, 121–2, 126
Aboriginals, 14, 20–5, 33, 81, 86, 87, 142, 143–4
    art, 25, 57, 83, 84–5, 95, 101, 115, 116, 118, 126, 131–2, 136–7, *168*, 177–8 *see also* Namatjira, Albert
        buying, 56, 57
        galleries, 177–8
    artefacts, 21, 95, 133
    communities, 47, 79, 99, 115, 116, 130–1, 133, 139, 154
        alcohol restrictions, 47, 85
        visiting, 47
    cultural tours, 181
    Dreaming lore, 77, 83, 86, 91, 94, 98, 101, 119, 120, 131, 148, 149
    Dreamtime, 16, 20
    groups
        Alyawarr, 146
        Anangu, 15, 20, 25, 31, 116
        Arrernte, 30, 31, 98, 100, 101
        Eastern Arrernte, 132
        Gurindji, 24
        Kaytetye, 146
        Ngaanyatjara, 22
        Pintubi–Luritja, 22
        Pitjantjatjara, 22
        Southern Arrernte, 15, 25
        Wakaya, 146
        Warumungu, 146
        Western Arrernte, 79, 83, 84, 90
        Yankunytjatjara, 22
    languages, 21–3
    sacred and significant sites, *47*, 69, 90, 94, 98, 100, 101, 126, 131–2, 144, 149
    tourism, 14–15, *24*, 25
Adelaide House, 27, 54, 56, 59
Afghans, 30, 60, 132
Aileron Hotel Roadhouse, 143
Albert Namatjira Gallery, 59
Alice Springs, 15, 26, 28, 30, 32, 52–73, 67, 87
Alice Springs Cultural Precinct, 59
Alice Springs Desert Park, 15, 61, *175*
Alice Springs Heritage Precinct, 67
Alice Springs Memorial Cemetery, 60
Alice Springs Old Courthouse, 68
Alice Springs Orogeny, 18
Alice Springs Telegraph Station, 26, 28, *52*, 92
Alice Springs Telegraph Station Historical Reserve, 62
Alice Springs, Visitor Information Centre, 54
Amadeus Sea, 114, 146
Anangu Tours, 118, 122
Anderson, Keith, 60
Angkerle Aboriginal Corporation, 92
Ants, 34
Anzac Hill, 56, 63
Apatula, 47, 130–1, 139
Araluen Centre for Arts and Entertainment, 59
Arid Australia Reptile Display, 65
Arid Zone Research Institute, 80
Arltunga, 27, 30, 98, 102 *see also* Gold
Arltunga Bush Hotel, 98
Arltunga Historical Reserve, 99–100
Atitjere Store *see* Harts Range
Australian crake, 83

Australian Inland Mission, 59
Aviation, 28, 29, 31, 60
Aviation Museum, 59, *60*
Ayers, Henry, 118
Ayers Rock, 27 see also Uluru
Ayers Rock Helicopters, 114, 115

Ballooning, *180*
Bardon, Geoffrey, 57
Barkly Highway, 155
Barrow Creek, *141*, 143–4
Battarbee, Rex, 85
Battery Hill Regional Cente, 157
Bicycle path, 92
Bilby, 37
Birds, 36–7, 91, 123
Birdwatching, 145
Black swan, 37, 83
Black-footed rock-wallaby, 34, 36, 37, 92, 105
Bloodwood, 33
Boggy Hole, 80, 81, 83
Bond Gap, 92
Bond Springs Airstrip, 144
Bond Springs Outback Retreat, 144–5
Bonney Creek, 147
Boulia, 154
Boxhole Meteorite Crater, 145–6
Breakaways, 158
Brumby, 37
Budgerigar, 36
Burrowing frogs, 32–3
Bush tucker, 33, 95, 119
Bushwalking, 39–40, 78–9, 80, 147, 173–4

CAAMA, 25
Camel, 30, 37, 41, 110, 143, 166
Camel Museum, 65
Camel Outback Safaris, 109–10
Camel races, 109 see also Lions Camel Cup
Carmichaels Crag, 126
Caruana, Wally, 57
Castle Rock, 131

Cat, 37
Cattle, 111
Central Australia, 12–13
    flora and fauna 32–7
    geology, 16–20, 108, 114, 136, 143, 146, 157
    history
        Aboriginal, 20–5
        European, 26–31
Central Australian Museum, 112
Central hare-wallaby, 37
Central Land Council, 25, 47, 83, 139
Central Mount Stuart, 136, 146
Central Mount Stuart Historical Reserve, 146
Central rock-rat, 88
Centralian flannel flower, 76–7, 92
Chambers Pillar, 133, 135, 139
Chambers Pillar Historical Reserve, 131
Charlotte Waters, 130
Charlotte Waters Telegraph Station, 134
Chateau Hornsby Winery, 63, 65
Chauvel, Charles, 112
Chewings Range, 89
Clark, Mac, 133, 135
Clark, Molly, 68, 134–5
Climate, 15, 32, 48–9
Cloncurry, 59
Communications, 15, 25, 49–51 see also Overland Telegraph, RFDS, School of the Air
Connellan, Eddie, 29, 31, 59, 60, 116
Connellan Airways/Connair, 29, 116
Conway, Ian and Lyn, 112–4
Coolibah, 36
Coolibah woodlands, 158
Cormorant, 37
Corroboree Rock, *101*
Corroboree Rock Conservation Reserve, 100
Cotterill family, 13, 29, 30, 112
Cox, Philip, 127
Crimson chat, 36
Currency exchange, 48
Curtin, John, 110

Curtin Springs Roadhouse, 115
Curtin Springs station, 12, 15, 110–11, 114–15
Cycad, 36, 77, 86, 92
Cycling, 41
Cypress, 149

Dalhousie homestead, *159*
Dalhousie Springs, 157, *159*
Darwin Overland Maintenance Force, 30
Date Gardens, The, 64–5
Davenport morning glory, 147
Davenport Range, 17, 146
Davenport Range NP, 146–7, 157
Desert bandicoot, 37
Desert Oaks Motel *see* Eridunda
Desert ranges, 32, 36
Devils Marbles, 13, 17, *19*, 31, *143*, 157
Devils Marbles Conservation Reserve, 147–8, 150
Dingo, 105, 110, 143
Dneiper station, 146
Dolomite Walk, 83
Dragon lizards, 33, 34
Drives, scenic, 174
Driving tips, 45–6
Drover's Boy, The, 72

East MacDonnell Ranges, 98–105, 162–3
Egan, Ted, 72
Ellery Creek, 19, 81
Ellery Creek Big Hole, 83
Email services, 51
Emergencies, 48
Emily and Jesse Gaps Nature Park, 100–1
Emily Gap, 2, 98, *101*
Emu, 33, 143
Equipment hire, 51
Eridunda, 111
Ernest Giles Road, 109
Essential information, 48–51
Euro, 101, 123
Events, 175–7
Everlasting, 33
Ewaninga, 21

Ewaninga Rock Carvings Conservation Reserve, 131–2
Fat-tailed antechinus, 37, 76
Ferns, 92
Finke *see* Apatula
Finke, William, 78
Finke Gorge, 77
Finke Gorge NP, 80–1, 89, 91, 108
Finke River, 19, 26, 37, 78, *80*, 81–3, 108, 114, 139, 157
    4WD Route, 91
Fish, 33, 83, 147
Flash floods, 104
Flynn, John, 29, 59, 71
    grave, 31, 59, 92
Forrest, John, 29
Forster Range, 144
Fossicking, 40–1, 104, 148, 154, 157
Four-wheel-driving, 40
Fox, 37
Fox, (..), 104
Frew River, 147
Frontier Camel Farm, 65–6
    Museum, 65
Frontier Services Museum, 56, 59 *see also* Adelaide House
Fullerton, Noel, 30, 109
Further afield, 152–9

Galah sessions, 72
Garden of Eden, 122, 125
Gargan, Michelle and Crispin, 109–10
Gecko, 33, 34
Gemstones, 102, 104, 148, 154 *see also* Fossicking
Gemtree, The, 148, *149*
General Motors' Sunraycer, 145
Geographical Centre of Australia, 136, 146
George Gill Range, 122, 169
Ghan, The, 28, 30, *43*, 132, *179 see also* Old Ghan
Ghost gum, *35*, 36, *97*, *162*, 101, 125, *171*
Ghost Gum Lookout, 88

Gibber country, 158
Gibson, Alfred, 27–8
Gibson Desert, 29
Giles, Alfred, 131
Giles, Ernest, 26, 27–8, 29, 79, 90, 114, 120–1, 131
Giles Springs, 86
Giles Track, 126
Glen Annie Gorge, *102*, 104
Glen Helen Gorge, 78, *82*, 83, 165
Glen Helen homestead, 83
Glen Maggie Homestead, 149
Glen of Palms, 27, 79 *see also* Finke Gorge
Goanna, 33
Gold, 27, 30, 99, 102, 142, *154*, 155, 157
Gondwana, 17, 81
Gosse, William, 27, 118, 120, 149
Gosse Bluff *see* Tnorala
Gosse Bluff Meteor Crater, *75*
Grey-crowned babbler, 34
Grey shrike-thrush, 37
Grey teal, 83
Guides, multilingual, 49
Guth, Henk, 70

Haasts Bluff, 83
Haasts Bluff Road, 83
Habitats, 32, 36
  desert ranges, 32
  mulga woodland, 32
  sandplain, 32
Hale River, 37, *102*, 104
Hann Range, 149
Hartley Street School, 66
Harts Range, 154, 155
Harts Range Store, 154 *see also* Aboriginal communities
Heavitree Gap, 66
Heavitree quartzite, 88
Heavitree Range, 89, 91
Henbury Meteorites Conservation Reserve, 19, 109, 111–12
Henley-on-Todd Regatta, 66–7
Hermannsburg (Ntaria), 23, 27, 30, 84–5, 90
Hermannsburg Sandstone, 136
Hitchcock, Bobby, 60
Honda solar vehicle, 145
Honey ants, 33
Hornsby, Denis, 65
Horseriding, 41
Hospitals, 48
Hot-air ballooning, 38
Hugh River, 19, 37, 81
Hummock grass, 34 *see also* Spinifex

Ian Barker's Sation Tours, 110, 115
Ice ages, 17, 19
Ikuntji Women's Centre, 83
Illamurta Springs, 91
Illamurta Springs Conservation Reserve, 85–6
Impaarja, 25
Impact craters, 94 *see also* Meteorite
Inarlanga Pass, 84, 87, 91
Information Centres, 172
Ininti Souvenirs and Cafe, 122
Interpreters *see* Guides, multilingual
Introduced animals, 37

James Ranges, 136
Jedda, 112
Jesse Gap, 21
Jim's Place, 112
John Flynn Memorial Church, 59
John Flynn Memorial Museum, 59
John Flynn's Grave Historical Reserve, 59, 92
John Hayes Rockhole, 105
Joint Defence Facility Pine Gap, 31, 95

Kalarranga Lookout, 86, *183*
Kantju Gorge, 119
Karingana, 121
Karu Lookout, 121
Kata Anga Tearoom, 85
Kata Tjuta, *4*, 13, 16, 18, 108, 120–1
Kathleen Springs, 125, 126
Kempe, Hermann, 27

Kilgariff, Joe, 144
Kimberley, 155
Kings Canyon, 13, 26, 27, 30, 108, 122, 124–6, 166–9
Kings Canyon Resort, 123, 126
Kings Canyon Walk, 112, 125
Kings Creek, 122, 125
Kings Creek Station, 112–14, 123
Kintore, 47
Kngwarreye, Emily Kane, 57
Knight, Jim, 60
Kookaburra tragedy, 60
Kulgera, 132–3, 139
Kulgera Hotel–Motel, 132
Kurundi station, 147

Lake Amadeus, 13, 27, 29, 114, 115
Lake Hopkins, 114
Lake Nash station, 155
Lake Wycliffe, 151
Lambert Centre, 136
Langford, Andrew, 62
Larapinta Drive, 78, 79
Larapinta Trail, 79–80, 87, 88, 91, 92
Lasseter, "Howard B.", 60, 110
Lasseter Highway, 108, 110
Lasseters Hotel Casino, 67
Lesser bilby, 139
Lherepirnte *see* Finke R.
Lilla Aboriginal Tours, 126
Lions Camel Cup, 67–8
Little Flower mission, 99
Long-tailed dunnart, 88
Lost City, 122, 125
Luritja Drive, 108–9
Lutheran Church, 23, 30, 84

Mac Clark Conservation Reserve, 133
MacDonnell, Richard, 77
MacDonnell Ranges, 13, *16*, 18, 30, 32, 36, *55*, 77–8 *see also* East and West MacDonells
MacDonnell Siding, 69, 73
Major Attractions, 172–3
Mala, 37

Maps
air routes, 42
Alice Springs CBD, 53, 55
Alice Springs environs, 58
Alice Springs Telegraph Station, 63
Arltunga Historical Reserve, 100
Davenport Range NP (prop.), 146
East MacDonnell Ranges, 97, 98
East MacDonnells tour, 163
European history, 28
Further afield, 153
Hermannsburg, 84
Kata Tjuta, 120
key to, 8
Kings Canyon, 125
Northern region, 141, 142
Palm Valley, 89
rail, 44
Red Centre, 6
road, 43
Serpentine/Inarlanga/Ochre Pits, 91
Simpsons Gap, 92
South-east region, 129, 130
South-west region, 107, 109
Trephina Gorge, 105
Uluru, 119
Uluru–Kata Tjuta, 117
Watarrka NP, 123
West MacDonnell Ranges, 76–7
West MacDonnells tours, 164
West of Alice Springs, 75
Witjira NP, 156, 157–8
Yulara/Kings Canyon, 167
Maruku Arts and Crafts, 122
Maryvale station, 133
McFarlane, James, 130
McGuires Road *see* Tanami Track
Media services, 49
Medicinal plants, 33
Mereenie Loop Road, 90, 94, 109
Mereenie oil and gas field, 109
Mereenie sandstone, 125
Meteorites, 19, *75*, 111–12, 145–6, 156
Meyers Hill, 69
Mica, 154

Missionaries, 27
Mistletoe bird, 37
Mobile phones, 49–50
Moon landings, 19
Motorbike tours, 83, 120
Mound springs, 157–8
Mt Conner, *12*, 13, 108, 111, 114–15, *116*
Mount Dare, 133–4, 157
Mt Ebenezer Roadhouse, 115
Mount Ervita, 73
Mt Gillen, 68
Mount Isa, 155
Mt Olga, 26, 27, 120 *see also* Kata Tjuta
Mt Palmer, 154
Mt Razorback, 87
Mt Sonder, 79, 87, 90
Mt Zeil, 13, 19, 78, 90
Mpaara Track, 86
Mpulungkinya Walking Track, 89
Mud Tank Zircon Field, 148
Mueller, Ferdinand von, 90
Mulga, 32
Mulga woodland, 32, 143
Museum of Central Australia, 60–1

Namatjira, Albert, 28, 60, 84, 85, 87, 94
Namatjira Drive, 78, 79
Namatjira Monument, 87
National parks and reserves, 173
National Pioneer Women's Hall of Fame, 56, 68, *69*
Native fig, 101
Native fuchsia, 33
Native Gap Conservation Reserve, 149
Native Title, 31
Native tomato, 101
N'Dhala Gorge, 21
N'Dhala Gorge Nature Park, 101–2
New Crown station, 134
Nicker, Sam, 149
Northern region, 140–51
Northern Territory, 30, 31
Northern Territory Aero Medical Service, 59
Ntaria *see* Hermannsburg

Ochre Pits, 87, 91
Old Andado station, 13, 133–4, *172*
　Mother's Day fundraiser, 135
Old Ghan, 68–9, 73, 130, 132, 139
Old Police Station Waterhole, 147
Old Timers Folk Museum, 69
Olive Pink Botanic Garden, 68, 69–70
Oodnadatta, 29, 30, 59
Oodnadatta Track, 158
Ooraminna Bush Camp, *134*, 135
Orange Creek station, 112
Organ Pipes, 83
Ormiston Creek, 88
Ormiston Gorge, 78, 88
Ormiston Pound, 78, 89
Osprey, 83
Overland Telegraph Line, 23, 26, 27, 29–30, 37, 142, 143–4, 151, 157
Overnight Walkers Registration Scheme, 51, 80, 126

Pacific Heron, 83
Pacoota sandstone, 83
Palm Creek, 84
Palm Valley, 29, 31, 80, 81, 89–90, 109
Panorama Guth, 70
Papunya Tula paintings, 57 *see also* Aboriginal art
Parks Australia, 116
Pastoralism, 31
Pedal radio, 59
Pelican, *36*, 37
Perkins, Larry, 145
Permits and passes, 175
Petermann Orogeny, 17
Petermann Ranges, 17, 92, 110
Pied butcherbird, 37
Pied honeyeater, 36
Pink, Olive, 60, 68
Pioneer Womens Hall of Fame, *see* National
Pituri, 87
Plenty Highway, 154–5
Port Hedland, 29
Port Lincoln ringneck, 105

Priscilla, Queen of the Desert, 125
Public transport *see* Transport and travel
Pussy tails, 33
Pwerte Marnte Marnte, 15, 25

Queen Elizabeth II, 70
Queensland Department of Geographical Information, 136

Rabbit, 37
Rabbit Flat Roadhouse, 156
Railways, 26, 28, 30 *sse also* Ghan, The
Rainbow Serpent, 148
Rainbow Valley, *17*, 109, 136–7
Rainbow Valley Conservation Reserve, 136–7
Red cabbage palm, 36, 77, 79, 81, 89
Red kangaroo, 32, *122*, 123
Redbank Gorge, 78, 90–1, 94
Reptiles, 33, *36*, 105
Residency, The, 56, 70, *71*
River red gum, 36, 76, 92, 104, 154, *162*
Road trains, *46*, 73, 150
Road Transport Hall of Fame, 73, 150
Roe Creek, 92
Ross, John, 26, 131
Ross River Homestead, 102, *103*, *163*
Royal Flying Doctor Service, 15, 29, *51*, 59
Royal Flying Doctor Visitor Centre, *70*, 71
Royal Geographical Society of Queensland, 136
Rubies, 102, *103*, 103–4
Ruby Gap Nature Park, 102, 104
Running Waters, 91
Rwetyepme, 90
Ryan, Ned, 149
Ryan Well Historical Reserve, 149

Sand dunes, 19, 108, 134, 158
Sandover Highway, 155
Sandplain, 32
Sandy inland mouse, 37
Santa Teresa, 99, 139

School of the Air, 15, 71, *72*
Schwarz, Wilhelm, 27
Serpentine Chalet Bush Camp, 91
Serpentine Gorge, 87, 91
Services and information, 170–81
Severin family, 12, 110, 115
Shute, Nevil, 54
Simpson Desert, 13, *18*, 19, 78, 101, *129*, 133, 134, 157
Simpson Desert Loop, 130, 133, 139
Simpson Desert Regional Reserve, 158
Simpsons Gap, 37, 78, 92
Skink, 33
Smith, Dick, 60
Sonder, Otto W., 90
Sounds of Starlight Theatre, 62–3
South-east region, 128–39
Southern Wall Lookout, 125
South-west region, 106–27
Spearwood, 121
Spinifex hopping-mouse, 34, 37
Spinifex pigeon, 34, 165
Standley, Ida, 92
Standley Chasm, 87, 92–3
Stapleton, James, 143
Station stays/tours, 39, 114, 135, 144–5, 157
Strehlow, Ted, 84
Stripe-faced dunnart, 37
Stuart, 26 30, 55 *see also* Alice Springs
Stuart, John McDouall, 23, 26, 77, 78, 112, 131, 136, 146
Stuart Highway, 108, 109, 139, 146, 149, 150, *151*, 154, 157
Stuart Town Gaol, 56, 71–2
Stuarts Well, 112
Sturt's desert pea, *32*
Swimming, 38, 62, 83, 88, 90. 105, 111, 143, 145, 147, 150, 151

Tanami Desert, 17, 155
Tanami Track, 155–6
Tangentyere Council, 24
Tawny frogmouth, 123
Ted Egan Show, 72

Tennant Creek, 17, 146, *153, 154,* 157
Termites, 34, 156
Tholstrup, Hans, 145
Thorny devil, 33–4, 36
Ti Tree, 26
Ti Tree Roadhouse, 150
Tjapaltjarri, Billy Stockman, 57
Tjupurrula, Johnny Warangkula, 57
Tnorala (Gosse Bluff) Conservation Reserve, 19, 90, 94
Todd, Alice, 30, 55
Todd, Charles, 30, 54, 144
Todd River, 27, 30, 37
Top End, 143, 155
Tour operators, 178–9
    Aboriginal culture, 181
    air, 179
    special interests, 179–80
Tour suggestions, 160–9
Tourism, 12–13, 29, 30–1, 112
    Aboriginal. 14–15, *24*
Traeger, Alfred, 59
Transitional environment zone, 146
Transport and travel, 42–7, 178
    Aboriginal lands, permits, 47
    air, 42, *45*
    bookings, 42–5
    bus, 42–3
    car, 44
    driving tips, 45–6
    organised tours, 44–5
    rail, 43
    road information, 46
Transport Heritage Centre, 73
Trephina Gorge, 21, *97, 162*
Trephina Gorge Nature Park, 104–5
Tropic of Capricorn, 144
Tuit, Len, 29, 91
Twin ghost gums, 94
Tylers Pass Lookout, 94

Uluru, *10,* 12, 13, 16, 18, 21, 25, 27, 29, 31, 108, 116, *117,* 118–20
Uluru Experience, 115, 118
Uluru–Kata Tjuta Cultural Centre, 116, 118, 121–2
Uluru–Kata Tjuta NP, 12, 31, 116, 118
Umbrella bush, 122
UFOs, 143, 151 *see also* Wycliffe Well
Using this guide, 8–9

Valley of the Winds Walk, 121
Vegetation, 91, 122, 147
Visiting Aboriginal communities, 47

Waddywood, 133
Wallaby, 33, 34
Wallaby Gap, 80
Wallace Rockhole, 95, *168*
Wallara Ranch, 112
Walpa Walk, 121
Warburton, Peter E., 29
Warburton, Richard, 29
Watarrka NP, 14–15, 20, 36, 90, 91, 108, 109, 122–3
Waterpenny, 91
Wauchope, 150–1
Wave Hill station, 24
Wedge-tailed eagle, 100, 143
West MacDonnell NP, 31, 77, 78–80
West MacDonnell Ranges, 74–95, 164–5
Whistleduck Creek, 147
White-striped mastiff bat, 34
Wildlife, 15, 33, 37, 76, 83, 88, 101, 110, 116, 122–3, 143, 147
    observing, 34
Wiltshire, Henry, W., 81
Witchetty grub, 33
Witjira NP, 133, 157
Wolfe Creek Meteorite Crater, 156
Wolfram, 150
Woodland Trail, 92
World Solar Challenge, 145
World War II, 29, 30, 99, 142
Wycliffe Well, 143, 151

Yaperlpe *see* Glen Helen Gorge
Yellow-top daisy, 33
Yuendumu, 47
Yulara, 12–13, 31, 116, 127, 166–9

Contents

About the guide	8
INTRODUCTION	10
Overview: The Red Centre	12
Landscape and Geology	16
Aboriginal History	20
European History	26
Plants and Animals	32
Activities	38
Getting There and Getting Around	42
Essential Information	48
ALICE SPRINGS	52
WEST OF ALICE SPRINGS	74
EAST OF ALICE SPRINGS	96
SOUTH-WEST OF ALICE SPRINGS	106
SOUTH-EAST OF ALICE SPRINGS	128
NORTH OF ALICE SPRINGS	140
FURTHER AFIELD	152
SUGGESTED TOURS	160
East MacDonnell Ranges	162
West MacDonnell Ranges	164
Yulara and Kings Canyon	166
REFERENCE DIRECTORY	170
INDEX	182